Liverpool Everyman and Playhouse present the world première of

The Electric Hills

BY MICHAEL MCLEAN

First performed on 9 March 2007 at the Everyman Theatre, Liverpool

Sponsored by

Liverpool Everyman And Playhouse

About The Theatres

As Liverpool prepares to take on the mantle of European Capital of Culture in 2008, the Everyman and Playhouse are experiencing a dramatic upsurge in creative activity. Since January 2004, we have been continually in production, creating shows which have ensured that 'Made In Liverpool' is widely recognised as a stamp of theatrical quality once again.

Around our in-house productions, we host some of the finest touring companies from around the country, to offer a rich and varied programme for the people of Liverpool and Merseyside, and for the increasing number of visitors to our city.

But there is more to these theatres than simply the work on our stages. We have a busy Literary Department, working to nurture the next generation of Liverpool Playwrights. A wide-ranging community department takes our work to all corners of the city and surrounding areas, and works in partnership with schools, colleges, youth and community groups to open up the theatre to all.

Our aim is for these theatres to be an engine for creative excellence, artistic adventure, and audience involvement; firmly rooted in our community, yet both national and international in scope and ambition.

'The two theatres have undergone a remarkable renaissance...
Liverpool's theatreland has not looked so good in years' Daily Post

13 Hope Street
Liverpool
L1 9BH
www.everymanplayhouse.com
Company Registration No. 3802476 Registered Charity No. 1081229

Liverpool Everyman and Playhouse would like to thank all our current funders:

Corporate members

AC Robinson and Associates, Barbara McVey, Beetham Organisation, Benson Signs, Brabners Chaffe Street, Chadwick Chartered Accountants, Concept Communications, Downtown Liverpool in Business, Duncan Sheard Glass, DWF Solicitors, EEF Northwest, Grant Thornton, Hope Street Hotel, Lewis's, Lime Pictures, Lloyds TSB Corporate Markets, Mando Group, Morgenrot Chevaliers, Radio City 96.7, Synergy Colour Printing, The Mersey Partnership, Victor Huglin Carpets.

Trusts and Foundations

The PH Holt Charitable Trust, The Eleanor Rathbone Charitable Trust, The Granada Foundation, The Lynn Foundation, The Peggy Ramsey Foundation, The Liverpool Culture Company, The Rex Makin Charitable Trust, The Golsoncott Foundation, The Pilkington General Fund, The Harry Pilkington Trust, The Garrick Trust, The Julia Marmor Trust, The Ernest Cook Trust, The Vandervell Trust, The Kobler Trust, The Penny Cress Charitable Trust, Malcolm and Roger Frood in memory of Graham and Joan Frood, The Helen Hamlyn Foundation, E Alec Coleman Charitable Trust, Duchy of Lancaster Benevolent Fund.

And our growing number of individual supporters.

NEW WRITING AT THE LIVERPOOL EVERYMAN AND PLAYHOUSE

'The Everyman is back producing the next generation of Liverpool playwrights' The Guardian

At the beating heart of the theatre's renaissance is our work with writers; since it is our passionate belief that an investment in new writing is an investment in our theatrical future.

Michael McLean has been part of the theatres' varied Playwright Support programme for over four years. A graduate of the Theatres' Young Writers Programme, he went on to receive readings of his work as part of the Everyman's annual new writing festival, Everyword, before being one of three writers invited to take part in the Henry Cotton Writers on Attachment Scheme.

The Electric Hills is the latest in a rich and varied slate of world, European and regional premières which has been enthusiastically received by Merseyside audiences and helped to put Liverpool's theatre back on the national map.

'The Everyman in Liverpool is living up to its name. Thanks to a new play, it is doing what theatres all over the country dream of: pulling in scores of first time theatre goers alongside loyal subscribers... blazes with energetic intelligence... this will change people's minds and in unexpected ways' The Observer on *Unprotected*

In just over two years, the theatres will have produced ten world premières of plays developed and nurtured in Liverpool – most recently including *The Flint Street Nativity* by Tim Firth, *The Way Home* by Chloë Moss, *Paradise Bound* by Jonathan Larkin and *Unprotected* by Esther Wilson, John Fay, Tony Green and Lizzie Nunnery, which transferred to the Edinburgh Festival where it won the Amnesty International Freedom of Expression Award.

'A remarkable renaissance' Liverpool Daily Post

Other highly acclaimed productions have included the European première of *Yellowman* by Dael Orlandersmith, which transferred to Hampstead Theatre and successfully toured nationally, and regional premières of Conor McPherson's *Port Authority*, Simon Block's *Chimps* and Gregory Burke's *On Tour* – a co-production with London's Royal Court Theatre.

As we prepare to celebrate European Capital of Culture in 2008, the Theatres have a variety of exciting projects in development which grow on the foundations of recent work.

'A stunning theatrical coup' Liverpool Echo on *Unprotected*

Around the main production programme, the theatres run a range of projects and activities to create opportunities and endeavour to support writers at every career stage. The commissioning programme invests in the creation of new work for both the Everyman and Playhouse stages.

The Young Writer's Programme is a year-long programme working alongside experienced practitioners, which nurtures and develops exciting new voices to create a new generation of Liverpool writers. An annual new writing festival, Everyword, offers a busy and popular week of seminars, sofa talks and work-in-progress readings.

'A rare play that captures the essence of Liverpool and its people without plunging into the usual clichés' Liverpool Daily Post on *Paradise Bound*

For more information about the Everyman and Playhouse – including the full programme, off-stage activities such as Playwright Support, and ways in which you can support our investment in talent – visit:
www.everymanplayhouse.com

CAST

(in alphabetical order)

Ricky Louis Emerick
Richard Dave Fishley
Joanne Claire Keelan
Kelisha Azuka Oforka

COMPANY

Writer Michael McLean
Director Nick Bagnall
Designer Becs Andrews
Lighting Designer Prema Mehta
Sound Designer Fergus O'Hare
Music Marc McLean
Costume Supervisor Marie Jones
Casting Director Kay Magson CDG
Dialect Coach Samantha Mesagno
Fight Director Kate Waters
Production Manager Emma Wright
Stage Manager Sarah Lewis
Deputy Stage Manager Roxanne Vella
Assistant Stage Manager Helen Wilson
AV Design Marc Williams
Lighting Operators Andrew Webster, David Sherman
Sound Engineer Marc Williams
Stage Crew Howard Macaulay
Set Construction Splinter
Dramaturg Suzanne Bell

Thank you to Cains for their support of Everyman and Playhouse press nights; Peter Hogart at Merseytravel; Mark from props at Hollyoaks; Dean Pendleton at LIPA; Joan Nice at Merseyrail; Elizabeth Anionwu; T-Mobile; Carphone Warehouse; Jean Hunt from Physio at The Royal Liverpool Hospital.

CAST

Louis Emerick Ricky

Louis's theatre credits include:
Master Harold & The Boys and *Ma Rainey's Black Bottom* (Liverpool Playhouse); *Little Pinch of Chilli* (Liverpool Everyman); *Basil & Beattie* (Manchester Royal Exchange); *The Liverpool Boat* (Dockers Club Belfast); *Sizwe Bansi Is Dead* (New Vic, Newcastle Under Lyme); *Jack & The Beanstalk* (Princess Theatre, Torquay); *Hamlet* (Horseshoe Theatre) and *The Resistible Rise of Arturo Ui* (Contact Theatre, Manchester).

Television credits include: *Brookside, Last of The Summer Wine, Casualty, Mile High, Floodtide, Doctors, Holby City, Merseybeat, The Bill, Cold Feet,* Presenter on *Granada Lunchtime Live, Albion Market, Home To Roost* and *Ball Trap On The Cote Sauvage.*

Film credits include: *Layer Cake* and *Fruit Machine.*

Dave Fishley Richard

Dave's theatre credits include:
The Odyssey (Lyric Hammersmith, Bristol Old Vic and tour); *Macbeth* (Out of Joint world tour); *Paradise Lost* (Bristol Old Vic); *Marat/Sade* (National Theatre); *A Special Relationship* (York and tour); *Dido, Queen of Carthage* (Shakespeare's Globe); *Crime and Punishment In Dalston* (Arcola Theatre); *Caledonian Road* (Almeida Theatre); *The Nativity* (Young Vic); *Twelfth Night* (Nuffield, Southampton); *Eritrea The Other War* (West Yorkshire Playhouse); *Silver Face* and *Ballad of Wolves* (Gate Theatre); *Now You Know* (Hampstead Theatre); *The Tempest* (Battersea Arts Centre); *Asylum! Asylum!* (Abbey Theatre Dublin); *Smoke* (Manchester Royal Exchange) and *Macbeth* and *The Tempest* (English Stage Company world tour).

Television credits include: *Casualty, Judge John Deed, The Bill, A Touch of Frost, Macbeth, Between The Lines* and *Buried* which won the BAFTA Award for Best Drama Series

Film credits include: *Bridget Jones' Diary, If Only, The Fifth Element* and *Solitaire For Two.*

Claire Keelan Joanne

Claire's theatre credits include: *Top Girls* (Diorama); *Ultra Violet* (Royal Court); *Les Liaisons Dangereuses* (Mary Wallace); *Rise and Shine* (Ebury Bridge) and *A Midsummer Nights Dream* (Canal Studio).
Television credits include: *Perfect Day*, *Sorted*, *Nathan Barley* and *The Arts Programme*.
Film credits include: *Pierrepoint*, *A Cock and Bull Story* and *Hard To Swallow* (short film).

Azuka Orforka Kelisha

Azuka trained at the Academy of Live and Recorded Arts.
Azuka's theatre credits include: *Skyvers* (Royal Court); *The Day of all Days* (Flight 5065/London Eye Project) and *'Low Dat* (Birmingham Rep).
Television credits include: *The Bill* and *Casualty*.
Training credits include: *Beautiful Thing*, *Twelfth Night*, *The Winter's Tale* and *Orpheus Descending*.

COMPANY

Michael McLean Writer

Litherland-born Michael was a finalist in the 2003 BBC New Comedy Awards for sketch writing at the Edinburgh Festival. His sketch was broadcast on BBC Three. Soon after, he joined the Everyman's Young Writers Programme, during which time he was invited to attend residential workshops with the London Royal Court Theatre.
His first play, *Joy Above*, was given a rehearsed reading at the Liverpool Everyman as part of Everyword 2005. *The Electric Hills* was written while Michael was one of three Henry Cotton writers on attachment at the Everyman and Playhouse in 2005 and lead to readings of the play in the summer of 2006 at both the Everyman and Soho theatre in London.
His radio play, *No Timewasters,* was written for the BBC Stages of Sound project and was broadcast in November 2006. He is currently developing projects with Lime Pictures and BBC Radio Drama.

Nick Bagnall Director

Nick's directing credits include: *Promises and Lies: The UB40 Musical* (Birmingham Rep); *Low Dat* and *Bolthole* (The Door, Birmingham Rep); *The Ruffian on The Stair* (Old Red Lion, London); *Mongoose* (Hoxton Hall and The Assembly Rooms, Edinburgh) and *Road* (Harrogate College of Arts and Technology).
Nick is co-founder of Sweetheart Production and is currently developing *The Late Nite Jeffrey Dahmer* by Wayne Leonard for

production later in the year.
Nick has also worked extensively as an actor in many theatres around the country. He was most recently seen in *The Flint Street Nativity* at the Playhouse and has also appeared at the Everyman in *The Mayor of Zalamea*.

Becs Andrews Designer

Theatre designs include: *Jeff Koons* (Actors Touring Company); *Twelfth Night* (English Touring Theatre); *Orestes 2.0* (Guidhall School of Music and Drama); *Hamlet* (Al Bustan Festival, Beirut); *Our Kind of Fun* (Live Theatre, Newcastle); *Perpetua* (Latchmere Theatre) and *What Became of The Witch* (Theatre and Beyond).
Opera/Musical Theatre designs include: *The Tinder Box* (Unity Theatre); *La Serva Padrona* (Linbury Studio, Royal Opera House); *Nabucco* (Riverside opera, Richmond); *The Magic Flute* (Opera Oxford) and *West Side Story* (Oxford Playhouse).
Dance/Physical Theatre designs include: *Set and Reset* (Edge Dance Company); *Lounge* (London Contemporary Dance School Studio); *Clepsydra* (Solas Dance Company); *Twos* (Juntos Dance Company) and *Corner of The World* (Brussels).
Becs won the 2003 Linbury Biennial Prize for Stage Design.

Prema Mehta Lighting Designer

Prema graduated from London's Guildhall School of Music and Drama.
Drama lighting designs include: *The Trouble with Asian Men* (Soho Theatre and national tour); *Year 10*

(Time Out Critics Choice, Mettre en Scène, Rennes and Théâtre National de Strasbourg); *Taking the Blood of Butterflies* (Oval Theatre); *Cariad* (Tristan Bates Theatre); *The Caucasian Chalk Circle* and *Top Girls* (Academy of Live and Recording Arts) and *Swingin' in Mid Dream* (Albany Theatre).
Dance designs include: *Solo*, *Moments* and *Ritual of Entrapment* (Purcell Room, South Bank Centre); *Spill* (semi-finals The Place Prize 2006) and The Robin Howard Dance Commission 2005 for *Parallels/ Dissonant/ Fine Line* (The Place and Lilian Baylis, Sadler's Wells).
Opera designs include: *Manon*, *The Rake's Progress*, *Semele*, *Hänsel und Gretel*, *Die Zauberflöte* and *Così fan Tutte* (Guildhall studio).
Prema was assistant to the Lighting Designer on *Death of a Salesman* (Lyric Theatre, Shaftesbury Avenue).

Fergus O'Hare Sound Designer

Fergus has worked on numerous productions for the National Theatre, Royal Shakespeare Company, Donmar Warehouse and the Old Vic.
Most recent work includes: *Our Country's Good* (Liverpool Playhouse); *The Entertainer* (The Old Vic); *The New Statesman* and *Rabbit* (Trafalgar Studios); *Whipping It Up* (Bush Theatre); *Improbable Frequency* (Traverse Theatre); *Fool For Love* and *Who's Afraid of Virgina Woolf?* (Apollo Theatre) and *See How They Run* (Duchess Theatre).
Work in New York, Los Angeles and Sydney includes: *Hecuba*, *The Shape of Things*, *A Day in the Death of Joe Egg*, *Dance of Death*, *Noises Off*, *An*

Enemy of the People and *Electra*, for which Fergus received a Drama Desk nomination.

Forthcoming credits will include: *Rabbit* at 59E59 in New York and *King Lear* and *The Seagull* with Ian McKellen directed by Trevor Nunn for the Royal Shakespeare Company.

Marie Jones
Costume Supervisor

Marie studied fashion and then moved on to Theatre Costume Interpretation at Mable Fletcher College. Marie's work as a freelance costumier has included costumes for Oldham Coliseum, The Royal Exchange, West Yorkshire Playhouse, Jimmy McGovern's film *Liam*, *Beyond Friendship* for Mersey Television and the creation of many panto dames who have appeared on the Everyman stage. She has worked extensively at the Everyman and Playhouse and has recently been employed full time as resident Wardrobe Supervisor. Most recently Marie's work here includes *Our Country's Good*, *The Flint Street Nativity*, *The Tempest*, *Unprotected*, *Billy Liar*, *Who's Afraid of Virginia Woolf?*, *Urban Legend*, *Fly*, *Breezeblock Park*, *The Entertainer*, *Still Life and The Astonished Heart*, *Ma Rainey's Black Bottom* and *The Anniversary*.

Marie's other credits include: *Brick Up the Mersey Tunnels* at The Royal Court, Brouhaha International Street Festival, Working Class Hero on the recent Imagine DVD, Costume Supervisor for many shows at LIPA, The Splash Project, for MYPT, and *Twopence to Cross The Mersey* at the Liverpool Empire.

Kay Magson CDG
Casting Director

Theatre credits include: *Ma Rainey's Black Bottom*, *Still Life and The Astonished Heart*, *The Odd Couple*, *Dr Faustus*, *Who's Afraid of Virginia Woolf?*, *Chimps*, *Season's Greetings*, *The Tempest*, *The Lady of Leisure*, *Billy Liar* and *The Flint Street Nativity* (Liverpool Playhouse); *Brassed Off* (Liverpool Playhouse and Birmingham Rep); *The Solid Gold Cadillac* (Garrick Theatre); *Dangerous Corner* (West Yorkshire Playhouse and West End); *Round The Horne... Revisited* (National tours); *Dracula* (Bromley and national tour); *Singin' In The Rain* (National tour); *Assassins* and *Shadowmouth* (Sheffield Theatres); *Follies* and *The Way of The World* (Northampton Theatres); *City of Angels* (English Theatre, Frankfurt); *A Model Girl* (Greenwich Theatre); *The Country Wife*, *Alfie: The Musical*, *Queen's English*, *One Last Card Trick*, *Blue Orange*, *Cinderella*, *Mother Goose* and *Aladdin* (Watford Palace Theatre); *The Yalta Disagreement* (Lincoln and West End); *Charley's Aunt* (Oxford Playhouse); *Private Lives*, *Master Class*, *Macbeth*, *The Importance of Being Earnest*, *Merrily We Roll Along* and *As You Like It* (Derby Playhouse); *Saved* (Bolton Octagon); *Old King Cole* (Unicorn); and *Caucasian Chalk Circle* and *Cyclops!* (Steam Industry for Scoop).

Kay was the resident Casting Director at West Yorkshire Playhouse for 17 years and is a member of the Casting Director's Guild of Great Britain.

STAFF

Leah Abbott Box Office Assistant, **Vicky Adlard** Administrator, **Laura Arends**, Marketing Campaigns Manager, **Deborah Aydon** Executive Director, **Jane Baxter** Box Office Manager, **Rob Beamer** Chief Electrician (Playhouse), **Lindsey Bell** Technician, **Suzanne Bell** Literary Manager, **Serdar Bilis** Associate Director, **Gemma Bodinetz** Artistic Director, **Emma Callan** Cleaning Staff, **Moira Callaghan** Theatre and Community Administrator, **Colin Carey** Security Officer, **Nicole Collarbone** Box Office Assistant, **Joe Cornmell** Finance Assistant, **Stephen Dickson** Finance Assistant, **Angela Dooley** Cleaning Staff, **Alison Eley** Finance Assistant, **Roy Francis** Maintenance Technician, **Rosalind Gordon** Deputy Box Office Manager, **Carl Graceffa** Bar Supervisor, **Mike Gray** Deputy Technical Stage Manager, **Helen Grey** Stage Door Receptionist, **Helen Griffiths** House Manager, **Jayne Gross** Development Manager, **Lesley Hallam** Stage Door Receptionist, **Talib Hamafaraj** Box Office Assistant, **Poppy Harrison** Box Office Assistant, **Stuart Holden** IT and Communications Manager, **David Jordan** Fire Officer, **Sarah Kelly** Assistant House Manager, **Sue Kelly** Cleaning Staff, **Steven Kennett** Assistant Maintenance Technician (Performance), **Sven Key** Fire Officer, **Lynn-Marie Kilgallon** Internal Courier, **Andrew King** Stage Door Receptionist, **Gavin Lamb** Marketing Communications Officer, **Rachel Littlewood** Community Outreach Co-ordinator, **Robert Longthorne** Building Development Director, **Howard Macaulay** Deputy Chief Technician (Stage), **Ged Manson** Cleaning Staff, **Christine Mathews-Sheen** Director of Finance and Administration, **Peter McKenna** Cleaning Staff, **Jason McQuaide** Technical Stage Manager (Playhouse), **Kirstin Mead** Development Officer, **Dan Meigh** Youth Theatre Director, **Liz Nolan** Assistant to the Directors, **Lizzie Nunnery** Literary Assistant, **Vivian O'Callaghan** Youth Theatre Administrator, **Sarah Ogle** Marketing Director, **Sean Pritchard** Senior Production Manager, **Collette Rawlinson** Stage Door Receptionist, **Victoria Rope** Programme Co-ordinator, **Rebecca Ross-Williams** Theatre and Community Director, **Jeff Salmon** Technical Director, **Hayley Sephton** House Manager, **Steve Sheridan** Assistant Maintenance Technician, **David Sherman** Deputy Chief Technician (Electrics), **Jackie Skinner** Education Co-ordinator, **Louise Sutton** Box Office Supervisor, **Jennifer Tallon-Cahill** Deputy Chief Electrician, **Matthew Taylor** Marketing and Press Assistant, **Pippa Taylor** Press and Media Officer, **Marie Thompson** Cleaning Supervisor/Receptionist, **Scott Turner** Market Planning Manager, **Hellen Turton** Security Officer, **Paul Turton** Finance Manager, **Andrew Webster** Lighting Technician, **Marc Williams** Chief Technician (Everyman), **Emma Wright** Production Manager.

Thanks to all our Front of House team and casual Box Office staff.

Board Members:
Cllr Warren Bradley, Professor Michael Brown (Chair), Mike Carran, Michelle Charters, Rod Holmes, Vince Killen, Professor E Rex Makin, Andrew Moss, Roger Phillips, Sara Williams, Ivan Wadeson.

The regulations of Liverpool City Council provide that:
The public may leave at the end of the performance by all exit doors and all exit doors must at that time be open. Note: all Liverpool theatres can be emptied in three minutes or less if the audience leaves in an orderly manner.
All gangways, passages, staircases and exits must be kept entirely free from obstruction.
Persons shall not be permitted to stand or sit in any of the intersecting gangways or stand in any unseated space in the auditorium unless standing in such space has been authorised by the City Council.
SMOKING AND DRINKING GLASSES ARE NOT ALLOWED IN THE AUDITORIUM AT ANY TIME.
We would like to remind you that the bleep of digital watches, pagers and mobile phones during the performance may distract the actors and your fellow audience members. Please ensure they are switched off for the duration of the performance. You are strongly advised not to leave bags and other personal belongings unattended anywhere in the theatre.

Michael McLean

THE ELECTRIC HILLS

OBERON BOOKS
LONDON

First published in 2007 by Oberon Books Ltd
521 Caledonian Road, London N7 9RH

A catalogue record for this book is available from the British Library.

Cover artwork by Uniform

ISBN: 1 84002 732 0 / 978-1-84002-732-7

Characters

RICKY
male, 42, black

KELISHA
female, 17, black

JOANNE
female, 29, white

RICHARD
male, 39, black

for my parents

and for Catherine – mi fido di te

My grateful thanks to the following for all their help
in writing this play: Serdar Bilis, Robbie Boardman,
Gemma Bodinetz, Rachel Brogan, Jason Cashen,
Matthew Dunster, Kevin Harvey, Steven Killeen,
Jonathan Larkin, Roy McCarthy, Nick Moss, Lizzie
Nunnery, Nick Quinn, Claire Reid, C M Taylor, The
Henry Cotton Award, The Peggy Ramsay Foundation,
and to all my friends and family.

Thanks to all at the Everyman and Playhouse for the
hard work. Thanks to Louis, Dave, Claire and Azuka.
Special thanks to Suzanne Bell for all the help from day
one. And thanks to Nick for everything.

ACT ONE

SCENE ONE

A single sustained synth note is heard.

The sound of a noisy concert crowd fades up.

A bass drum thumps out a steady, mid-tempo 4/4 beat and the crowd clap along straight away – they've done this before.

Camera flashes can be heard and seen. We can just about make out a figure on the stage.

A hi-hat joins in on the off beat. Then congas.

A few whistles and whoops from the crowd.

A second sustained synth note slides in over the existing one to build the tension.

RICKY HILL is centre stage, alone with a microphone. His body stoops. He has his head down and his eyes are glazed over, deep in thought.

Bass stabs sit on top of the bass drum.

The song gets louder, ready to take off. The crowd acknowledges this.

Brightly-coloured lights suddenly pulse in time as the song kicks in – a full-blooded, electronic dancefloor classic with a meaty snare, staggered handclaps, compressed piano, chicken scratch guitar, synth strings and real bass.

A distinctive, instantly catchy synthesizer hook plays over everything.

Just as it feels right for the singing to start, the song is drowned out by a whoosh and the song has disintegrated in a flash.

Finally all we are left with is the echo of the sustained synth string, a minor note, as the lights shrink on RICKY.

April. Monday. 5.30 pm. Living room.

RICKY sits on the decaying sofa, in a daydream. The TV is on. A PA system is set up in the room.

RICKY: (*Over the microphone.*) One-two.

> *The front door is heard to open off. RICKY hides to the side of the sofa. He immediately holds his back in excruciating pain.*

> *KELISHA enters wearing headphones. She sits on the arm of the sofa and picks up the TV remote. RICKY emerges, holding a small*

gong, and creeps up to KELISHA extremely slowly. He is about to bang the gong.

KELISHA: Y'all right, Dad?

RICKY flings the gong onto the sofa.

RICKY: You musta seen me.

KELISHA: I could *hear* you. Puffing away. Is your back playing up today?

RICKY: No.

KELISHA: Join the gym, I'll go with ya.

Beat.

Why's the gong down anyway?

RICKY: Charity night this Thursday.

KELISHA: Is it karaoke?

RICKY: And bingo.

KELISHA: Eee!

RICKY: Joanne's kindly volunteered me.

KELISHA: The Big Comeback.

RICKY: Dunno what gear I'm meant to use.

KELISHA: Your old microphone working?

RICKY: Not very well. Test it.

He holds the mic to KELISHA. The microphone crackles.

KELISHA: No.

RICKY: (*Over the mic.*) Go on.

KELISHA: I don't wannoo!

RICKY: (*Over the mic.*) Just say a joke.

KELISHA: I don't know any good ones.

RICKY: (*Over the mic.*) One of mine then.

Beat.

(*Over the mic, jokey.*) Hurry up.

KELISHA: (*Over the mic.*) Tch. What…do you call…a bear with lots of money?

RICKY waits.

RICKY: (*Over the mic.*) I don't know, what do you call a bear with lots of money?

KELISHA thinks.

KELISHA: (*Over the mic.*) I've forgotten.

RICKY: (*Over the mic.*) Winnie-the-pools.

KELISHA: (*Over the mic.*) Winnie-the-pools.

RICKY removes a CD player from her bag. A crumpled up yellow flyer also drops out.

RICKY: What ya been listenin to anyway?

KELISHA: Oh, nothing much.

RICKY: Nothing *at all.* There's no CD.

KELISHA: Must be in my bag.

RICKY: So what's with the headphones?

KELISHA: I just…like to. So no one bothers me. Cranks on the bus and that.

RICKY: Would it not make sense to actually *listen* to some music?

KELISHA: I do, I just forgot before, that's all.

Beat.

RICKY: There's no batteries in either.

KELISHA: Dad will ya sod off!

RICKY: Language.

KELISHA: You should never root through a lady's bag, in case ya didn't know.

RICKY: I was *packing* your schoolbag for you not that long ago.

KELISHA: Well I'm not at school now, am I? It's a college, *adult* education.

RICKY unfolds the crumpled yellow flyer and reads.

Is that curry I can smell?

RICKY: Er…sure is.

KELISHA: Vegetarian?

RICKY: More or less.

Beat.

'Speke'?

KELISHA: What? Will you STOP going through my bag?

RICKY: If you wanna be paid as a *cook*, I'll give you money to make my tea every night.

KELISHA: It's not a cook. It's more...waitressing.

RICKY: You?

KELISHA: Maybe.

RICKY: In a grubby café?

KELISHA: It won't be grubby. It's at the airport.

RICKY: You'll *need* a plane to get all the way to Speke.

KELISHA: My bus goes straight there, that's where I found the flyer.

Beat.

Immediate start, no experience needed.

RICKY: That's why it's ten thousand, pro-rata.

KELISHA: What does 'pro-rata' mean?

RICKY: It's Latin for 'not really'.

KELISHA: Isn't that good money then?

RICKY: What do you need money for when you're still at school?

KELISHA: *College.* To pay for what I wanna do after.

RICKY: Oh right. 'Stratford.'

KELISHA: *Stafford.* Maybe, yeah.

RICKY: And what's wrong with Liverpool again?

KELISHA: Nothing, but I've told ya! My tutor reckons I should look at this one depending on my results. Says it's really good.

RICKY: Is that the tutor who looks like a Chinese Chuckle Brother?

KELISHA: Dad...

RICKY: Is it?

KELISHA: He looks nothing like a Chuckle Brother.

RICKY: Okay, the one *I* think looks like a Chinese Chuckle Brother?

KELISHA: He's not actually *Chinese*, by the way.

RICKY: Well…

KELISHA: Wish you'd take it seriously.

RICKY: Oh I take it *very* seriously. I'd just hate to see you come crashing down with a bang at some university, that's all.

KELISHA: Oh thanks very much! I haven't even been to visit the place yet!

RICKY: S'pose *I'd* have to go would I?

KELISHA: Er, no you would not.

RICKY: You can't go on your own!

KELISHA: Course I can. Or Jo might come.

RICKY: Why Joanne and not me?

KELISHA: Oh Dad leave it, please.

RICKY: Okay, I will leave it. But I'll tell you this, you are NOT wasting your time working for buttons in some dive.

KELISHA: But I could at least see –

RICKY: No way Kelisha. End of.

Beat.

Make yourself useful, ring Jo and ask her to grab a bag of chips if she's passing somewhere.

KELISHA dials on the house phone and sniffs.

You still got a cold?

KELISHA: Nah, it's nothing.

RICKY: I'll do you a hot orange. And this curry'll clear your sinuses. Probably be too spicy for a squirt like you?

KELISHA: As if. God, when we getting a new phone, Dad? Got to break your finger if there's a seven in the number.

RICKY: Soon.

A mobile phone starts ringing. The ringtone is the riff we heard in the opening song. RICKY picks up a mobile from behind the sofa. The front door is heard off and KELISHA moves over to look out.

KELISHA: Oh here she is now!

RICKY holds his back in pain again, which KELISHA doesn't see. He chucks the mobile and hides to the side of the sofa again. JOANNE enters. Her fleece has DIY-4-U MEGASTORE on the front. She walks straight in, fed up, and slumps down on the sofa.

Hiya Jo.

KELISHA kisses JOANNE.

JOANNE: Hiya.

KELISHA: Just phoned you.

JOANNE: Oh, have you? I didn't hear –

KELISHA: No, it's there.

JOANNE: Oh yeah. Useless anyway, no one ever rings me.

KELISHA: Aah, they do. I do. How was work?

JOANNE: Oh it was *fantastic.*

KELISHA: You book that day off for next week?

Beat.

For my open day?

JOANNE: Er…yeah, I will tomorrow.

KELISHA: Oh doesn't matter, honest.

JOANNE: No, course I will Kel. I'll book the train tomorrow.

RICKY's head pops up from the back of the sofa behind JOANNE. He is about to bang the gong.

Don't even think about it, knobhead.

RICKY stands and holds his back.

Been waiting there all day have you, Rigsby?

RICKY: Actually, I was just about to fetch a hot drink for my delicate little daughter who's got a cold.

KELISHA: I haven't.

JOANNE: Oh ey Kel, you just kissed me.

RICKY: Where's *my* kiss?

JOANNE gestures to her backside. As she does so, she retrieves something she's sat on.

JOANNE: What the hell's this?

KELISHA: Is it a pork pie?

RICKY: Oh, was lookin for that. Had a pack this morning, musta dropped one.

JOANNE: You had a packet of *pork pies* for breakfast?

RICKY: I had Coco Pops an' all like.

JOANNE: Put it in the bin.

RICKY eats it in one.

KELISHA: Eurgh!

KELISHA sits close to JOANNE, unties her hair.

Leave your hair down Jo, I've told ya!

JOANNE: It was doin me head in, it's a mess.

KELISHA: Where's your straighteners?

JOANNE: Bathroom.

KELISHA: Come up a sec, I'll get the kinks out.

RICKY: What are The Kinks doing in our bathroom?

Beat.

KELISHA: He's done us a curry.

JOANNE: Oh aye. Been watching cookery programmes?

RICKY: Is that what you think I do all day, watch telly?

JOANNE: I know for a fact you've been lying on this couch all afternoon in your undies, catching up on *Murder, She Wrote.*

RICKY: I have not! It was *Quincy* today.

JOANNE: Oh it's funny isn't it?

RICKY: What's up with your mush?

JOANNE: I've been working all day.

KELISHA: Can we *have* some chips then?

Beat.

RICKY: Got no change on me.

JOANNE: Here y'are. Seventy-four p. How much is a portion?

RICKY: Ninety. Just ask him for seventy-four pence worth.

JOANNE: Why don't we just ask them for credit while we're at it?

KELISHA: I've got some slummy in me money box.

JOANNE: You know what, just see if you can get a tenner out.

21

JOANNE holds her debit card out to KELISHA.

RICKY: You're already overdrawn on that aren't you?

Beat.

KELISHA: Right then, see you in bit.

KELISHA takes the card and exits.

RICKY: Careful up there, Kel!

KELISHA exits. RICKY goes to the front door, watching her leave.

When she came in before...

JOANNE: What?

RICKY: She had headphones on with no music.

JOANNE: How d'you know?

RICKY: I checked. She seemed embarrassed.

JOANNE: I'm not surprised! She's an adult.

RICKY: Seventeen.

JOANNE: Almost eighteen. Let her do her own thing.

RICKY: I do!

JOANNE: Some mates, that's what she needs.

RICKY: We're her *best* mates.

JOANNE: Exactly.

Beat.

RICKY: She wants to start working. Some café.

JOANNE: Good on her.

RICKY: She doesn't have to work.

JOANNE: We could do with the extra money if she did.

RICKY: I've told ya, I'll start looking for gigs.

JOANNE: I've heard that for the past eight years.

RICKY: Well she's not doing it. It's been decided.

JOANNE: By Kelisha?

Beat.

JOANNE stands up and goes to walk past RICKY. He touches her. She relaxes momentarily and puts her arms around him. She touches his back.

Want me to rub some Fiery Jack in?

RICKY: Nah.

JOANNE: (*Looks down.*) Is it stiff?

RICKY: Pardon?

Beat.

JOANNE: Right, I best get a bath before tea.

She goes to separate. RICKY tries to keep her and moves in for a kiss.

No, not now. I stink of varnish and paint and...sweat from running round after people all day.

JOANNE breaks.

RICKY: Leave the water in after.

JOANNE: You phoned the doctor's yet?

Beat.

RICKY: Do you fancy a quick go of the Yes/No game?

JOANNE: No.

RICKY bangs the gong.

JOANNE exits.

RICKY: (*Over the microphone.*) And try not to wee in the bath. My eyes were stinging last time.

RICKY sits down. He breathes out, only now able to stop hiding his pain.

He picks up the yellow piece of paper and reads it. He begins to carefully fold the paper.

The deep rumble of a plane speeding along a runway is heard.

RICKY pulls his arm back, holding a paper aeroplane. He throws it in front of him and we hear the sound of a plane taking off into...

SCENE TWO

Thursday (three days later). 6.30 pm. Airport café.

RICHARD is sitting at a table. He wears a large woolly hat. He is extremely still, like a mannequin. He stares ahead for a long time. Suddenly he blinks, scratches his head and he seems to be out of his trance. He turns to the next table, stares at it, decides to move to it.

He looks down at a page of a magazine and carefully begins to tear. He stops and notices an opened crisp packet on the adjoining table. He creeps over, then sees someone coming and rushes back to his chair, hiding the crisps.

KELISHA enters with disinfectant and cloths. She's a good few tables away. RICHARD stops what he's doing and stares at her. KELISHA seems tired but keen, breathing out, wiping her brow. She becomes aware of RICHARD's stare and looks over. RICHARD turns away quickly, caught out. KELISHA sprays and wipes a table. RICHARD starts tearing the paper again. The noise seems to worry him and he does it painfully slowly, which is worse. KELISHA looks towards him. He stops mid-tear and holds the paper still. Though his head is down his eyes are on her. KELISHA seems disturbed, possibly annoyed. She picks up her stuff and moves to a table even closer, but avoids eye contact.

RICHARD visibly tries to pluck up the courage to speak, his mouth open for a long period before the words come out.

RICHARD: Hel…hello. Hello again.

KELISHA nods slightly, fakes a smile.

Am I…um? Okay? Am I okay? Here? Am I okay *sitting* here?

Beat.

I mean, I've not bought anything. Off you.

KELISHA: 'S fine.

RICHARD: Thanks. If you can…if you're sure.

Beat.

Thank you.

KELISHA sprays the table and wipes.

Wiping 'ey?

Beat.

Doing a bit of the old wiping there.

KELISHA: Yeah.

RICHARD: Cool man. Don't think there was…wasn't much mess on that table though, was there?

Beat.

Still gotta clean it though?

KELISHA: Mm, every table.

RICHARD: *Every* table!?

RICHARD looks around.

Twenty-four.

KELISHA: Ey?

RICHARD: Twenty-four tables. Eight this way, three across. Twenty-four, isn't it?

KELISHA: Thanks for that.

RICHARD: Oh sorry, I didn't mean to…

Pause.

I could give you a touch.

KELISHA: A what?

RICHARD: Give you a hand, sweep the floor.

KELISHA continues wiping.

KELISHA: Machine does that.

Beat.

RICHARD: You're on your own here are you?

KELISHA: No. Not at all. Kitchen's closed. There's plenty about though. Security and that.

RICHARD: Right. So you're just a cleaner then?

KELISHA: No. I'm serving too. You can still buy stuff. Tea and coffee. Butties, crisps, cans and that. Snacks.

RICHARD: Oh right. Don't need the kitchen for that kind of thing really, do you? Just cold stuff.

Beat.

Apart from the tea and coffee!

Beat.

The tea and coffee…it's self-service, is it?

KELISHA: No.

RICHARD: Ah great!

Beat.

KELISHA: So do you want one or not?

RICHARD: Oh, no thank you. No, it's just… I hate it when it's self-service. I never know what to do. I start flapping. Aargh!

Beat.

The way there's never…instructions, just this big *thing* in front of you with all kinds of knobs and buttons and gaps. I mean, do you lift the cup up, press this, shove it under that…what? I get all…

Beat.

KELISHA: I know what you mean there, actually.

RICHARD: Do ya?

KELISHA: Yeah. There's been times in college I've wanted a cuppa from the machine but then panicked. So I usually just end up buying a bottle of Lilt.

RICHARD: I know *exactly* what you mean. It's mad innit!

Beat.

You're er…you're like me. Aren't ya?

Beat.

KELISHA continues wiping. RICHARD sees this as a defence against him and shrinks back down again, stares at his magazine.

Sorry.

Beat.

KELISHA: Are you okay?

RICHARD: Yeah yeah. You get back to your…wiping, I'm sorry to have disturbed your work.

Beat.

KELISHA: Don't worry about it.

Pause.

RICHARD: Any cigarette machines round here?

KELISHA: No idea.

RICHARD: Think they only take pounds. I've just got a few Euro coins on me. Newsagent's shut too. Do you know if it opens again soon?

KELISHA: Couldn't tell ya.

RICHARD: Get busier in the day, does it?

KELISHA: Started at five. Shuts at ten. Been dead.

RICHARD: Nice and peaceful though, ey?

KELISHA: Mm.

Beat.

That man's just had a go at me though.

RICHARD: Who, the guy in the suit?

KELISHA: Wanted a sausage toastie.

RICHARD: What did you say?

KELISHA: Said sorry, kitchen's closed. Just got normal butties.

RICHARD: Cold stuff.

KELISHA: Yeah. Exactly. He said 'How hard can it be to forage a sausage toastie in a cafe?'

RICHARD: *Forage?*

KELISHA: I know, don't even know what that means, do you?

RICHARD: No.

KELISHA: There's actually shedloads of sausages in the kitchen. It's me first night here. Apparently the cook leaves leftovers for the staff. And there's a huge great barrel of them today, you wanna see it.

RICHARD: Don't you want them?

KELISHA: I don't eat meat.

RICHARD: Never?

KELISHA: Not since I was ten.

RICHARD: Is that cos you think it's cruel?

KELISHA: S'pose.

RICHARD: Yeah. It is. I still eat meat though. Sorry.

KELISHA: 'S all right. My family do too.

RICHARD: All of them?

KELISHA: Well, both… You can use Euros in here, by the way. If you wanna buy anything.

RICHARD: Can you? I've got fourteen. Do you reckon you could swap them all?

KELISHA: Er…don't think I'm allowed. The till you see. Might cock it up.

RICHARD: Just need a ciggy before I get on the plane.

KELISHA: Can't help you with that, sorry. I don't smoke.

RICHARD: Oh no, I wasn't…I wouldn't dream of asking you. I'm not like that.

Beat.

KELISHA: Where you going?

RICHARD: Amsterdam.

KELISHA: On your hols, like?

RICHARD: I live there.

KELISHA: Honest? How long for?

RICHARD: Er…few years now, on and off.

KELISHA: On your own?

RICHARD: I stay with the people I work for.

KELISHA: Doing what?

RICHARD: In a…café.

KELISHA: Bit like me, then.

RICHARD: Yeah.

Pause.

KELISHA: You know…if you pay for something here with those Euros, I can give you change in English.

RICHARD: Oh. Well…what's the cheapest thing you can buy then?

KELISHA: Erm…it'll be a banana. No! Chomp, ten p.

RICHARD: Ten p? *Chomp.*

KELISHA: Yeah.

RICHARD: Can I buy *you* one? As a thanks.

KELISHA: Don't be daft.

RICHARD: No, I'm deadly serious.

KELISHA laughs slightly. RICHARD seems upset by this.

KELISHA: No, er…all right then. Cheers.

RICHARD: Erm…do you want me to come up…

KELISHA: Oh no, you can stay there, I'll bring it all over.

RICHARD: Cool man. Thank you.

KELISHA exits. RICHARD retrieves the crisp packet, crushes the packet, tilts his head and knocks them back in one. He continues carefully tearing at the magazine. KELISHA returns with two Chomps, a sandwich, crisps and a banana milkshake. She is whistling a tune as she approaches. It is the hook from the song at the beginning of the play.

KELISHA: Here we are.

RICHARD: What was that then?

KELISHA: What was what when?

RICHARD: That tune you were whistling?

KELISHA: Erm. Can't remember.

RICHARD whistles the tune. KELISHA joins in, smiling.

That's just…it's my dad's song, I was listening to it before on my headphones. Do you remember it?

RICHARD: Your dad?

KELISHA: Yeah. He was in a band.

RICHARD: Your dad?

KELISHA: Mm. Eighties. He's a bit…famous, I suppose. Only had one hit. That was it. Do you remember it?

Pause.

RICHARD: I do.

KELISHA: Do ya!? Were you into it like?

Beat.

Ah wow! I love it when this happens! Not that it does very often like, it's not like I brag or tell everyone about it. I'm not like that.

Beat.

Mad ey!?

Beat.

God…

Beat.

I'll have to tell him.

RICHARD: What?

KELISHA: That I met someone who knew it!

RICHARD: Is he coming here?

KELISHA: To be honest he doesn't know I'm working here. Haven't told him yet.

Beat.

No, it might cheer him up, reassure him he has got fans out there! Still does a bit, me dad. Not often. Does discos and that, and singing when he can. Hard for him. You know... 'showbiz'.

KELISHA checks her watch.

Right now, my dad'll be on his way to work at the very prestigious Seaforth Royal British Legion.

RICHARD: Where's that?

KELISHA: In Seaforth. It's a charity night. Showbiz, ey!

Beat.

Here. Nine pound fifty-five.

RICHARD: Oh.

KELISHA: That'll be enough. Won't it?

RICHARD notices the food.

RICHARD: What's all this, you having your break?

KELISHA: Oh. No. It's...it's all yours. If you want.

RICHARD: For me?

KELISHA: I'm allowed a sandwich, bag of crisps and a drink every shift.

RICHARD: Why aren't you having it?

KELISHA: I had a big tea. Couldn't eat anyway, the way people've been talking to me tonight.

KELISHA looks over to the other side of the café. RICHARD seizes this moment to re-group and we see him trying to calm himself: squeezing his fingers, gulping, breathing quickly etc. He does it just about subtly enough for KELISHA not to notice as she gets on with her cleaning. He picks up the sandwiches.

RICHARD: 'BLT.'

KELISHA: That okay?

RICHARD: Bacon.

KELISHA: Don't you like bacon? If you take it out it'll only be an LT! You could have an SLT.

RICHARD: What's that?

KELISHA: The S'd be sausage. Make our mate over there jealous!

Beat.

Not into sausages either? Don't worry, you wouldn't have to eat them *all!*

Beat.

You okay?

RICHARD: You're very kind.

KELISHA: Don't mention it.

Beat.

RICHARD: Is your dad proud of you?

KELISHA: Working in a café? Yeah he'll be dead proud!

RICHARD: He must be though.

KELISHA: Dunno. I'm studying. Got me exams in a few weeks. I wanna do drama. Or be a vet. Can't decide.

RICHARD: Which one would your dad prefer?

KELISHA: Doesn't say. Wish he would. When I ask him he just says why not combine the two and act the goat.

Beat.

Can't see me working here for long. Thought I'd be able to save up all summer. Feel stupid.

Beat.

Horrible people get in your way.

RICHARD: Oh.

KELISHA: I don't mean you. You're nice.

RICHARD: You're nice too.

Beat.

How old are you?

KELISHA: Why?

RICHARD: Do you like wine?

Beat.

KELISHA: Why?

RICHARD: There's a token here. In the magazine. 'Free bottle of wine. At participating off-licences. Worth four ninety-five.' Just need to bring the token.

He hands her the token he's been tearing.

Here. You have it.

KELISHA: Go 'way. It's yours.

RICHARD: As a thank you.

KELISHA: I've never even had wine.

RICHARD: Please.

KELISHA: Honest.

RICHARD: Go on.

KELISHA: You have it.

RICHARD: I don't really drink.

KELISHA: Neither do I.

RICHARD: I'm getting on the plane soon.

KELISHA: Just leave it then.

RICHARD: You could give it to someone.

KELISHA: No one to give it to.

RICHARD: Give it to your dad.

KELISHA: He wouldn't have it.

RICHARD: Please.

KELISHA: No.

RICHARD: Please.

KELISHA: No.

RICHARD: Please.

KELISHA: (*Beginning to laugh.*) No.

RICHARD: Please.

KELISHA: No.

RICHARD: Please.

KELISHA: No!

KELISHA picks up her stuff.

Thanks, but I'm fine.

She walks away.

Anyway, I wouldn't get served.

RICHARD: Why not?

KELISHA: I'm not eighteen.

KELISHA exits. RICHARD puts down the token.

RICHARD: Neither am I.

We hear the plucking of an acoustic guitar and a D major chord rings out into…

SCENE THREE

Thursday (two hours later). 8.30 pm. Seaforth British Legion.

As the chord rings out, a voice begins 'Help Me Make It Through The Night' by Kris Kristofferson.

The voice is RICKY's. The backing track is a cheap karaoke recording. He is singing on his radio mic away from the Legion stage, wandering round to test the acoustics. He eventually emerges, slowly strolling onto his stage confidently. He sings as though performing but after a few lines tails off, walks about, adjusts the PA, the odd 'tut' and 'one-two' on the mic. He lowers the volume.

RICKY: (*Over the microphone.*) Right ladies and gents. How we doing, are we ready for a good night?

No reply.

I said how we doing, are we ready for a good night?

A few pathetic shouts.

Well, I'm sure you'll agree we've got a real party atmosphere in here on this Thursday night in Seaforth. Just gonna give five minutes or so before we get going. Coming up in the interval we've got the raffle and the Irish bingo from Sid, after which the buffet will be open. Oh talking of which, I've been told to thank the lovely Ann and Pat from the Seaforth Bakery for the gala pie. Actually Pat, you might be able to help me with something, always bugged me…those long gala pies – how do you get a big long egg to go right through the middle?

He listens for the answer.

You'll tell me later?

He laughs.

Okay, put my mind at ease. Right then, the karaoke files should be doing the rounds, so if you're feeling brave, fill in a form…and I'll see you in a short while.

He stops the song and puts on some background music. He continues setting up his gear. JOANNE enters with a glass of lemonade for him and a pint of lager for her. She sits next to his gear and lights a cigarette.

JOANNE: Sid's in a panic. He's only sold twenty-odd raffle tickets. Says that doesn't even pay for first prize.

RICKY: What is first prize?

JOANNE: Set of power tools from our work.

RICKY: No wonder then.

JOANNE: It's a good prize that.

RICKY: Most of the people in here are in sheltered accommodation, they don't need to do-it-themselves.

JOANNE: You should buy some tickets. Our bedroom couldn't half do with a facelift.

RICKY: Nothing wrong with it.

JOANNE: Tatty ald cabinets.

RICKY: Meant to look like that. They're…*distressed.*

JOANNE: They're inconsolable by the looks of it.

RICKY: Not surprised the room looks grubby with your ciggy smoke all over it.

JOANNE: I don't smoke in the house!

RICKY: (*Impersonating JOANNE.*) 'I only smoke when I'm having a bevvy.'

Beat.

You heard off Kel?

JOANNE: No why?

RICKY: Just to see if she's all right, what she's up to.

JOANNE: She'll just be in her room. Got revision hasn't she.

Beat.

Nervous?

RICKY: I'm okay. Where's that disc gone?

RICKY bends down to root through one of his boxes.

JOANNE: Here y'are I'll get it.

RICKY: I'm all right, I've got it.

JOANNE: Bend with your *knees*, Ricky. Need to watch your back.

RICKY: It's fine. It's all right if I'm active, don't feel a thing.

JOANNE: Sid says all the committee fellas are impressed with ya.

RICKY: Haven't even started yet!

JOANNE: I know but just…your announcements, the way you set
up earlier with the staff and that. What was that fella saying to
ya by the bar?

RICKY: Wanted…an autograph.

JOANNE: Ha! Saddo! How did ya feel?

RICKY is genuinely sheepish.

Ah, well in hun! See?

RICKY: Just don't want anything going wrong, that's all.

JOANNE: Think you're a bit of a hit with the ladies too. Look at
that ald bird in her little trouser suit, well eyein' you up.

RICKY: Actually yeah, go and sit somewhere else.

JOANNE: She might think I'm your sexy backing dancer!

RICKY: Yeah, cos most dancers warm up with a Stella and a
Marlboro Light don't they?

JOANNE: Here's to a good gig anyway, hun. Cheers.

RICKY: Cheers.

*They touch glasses and drink. RICKY keeps busy setting up as they
talk.*

JOANNE: *Anyway*...get a load of this, Mr Superstar. You're not gonna be the only famous face in our house soon. *I* have just starred in a *television* commercial.

RICKY: You?

JOANNE: Oh yes. I'm doing the paint promotion.

JOANNE hands RICKY her pint and cigarette and kneels on the floor.

I had to say something like: 'We'll help you choose the right colours from our top-brand range of paints, and for every two litre enamel you buy, you get the second for...' I dunno, half-price or some shite...

RICKY: Right. Think that last bit needs a bit of work.

JOANNE: Sid's so funny, I'll get him to do his for you in a bit. Sid! Here a sec!

RICKY: Stand up Jo, anyone looking probably thinks you're proposing.

Beat.

You know, I mean...I'm not getting hitched to someone off the telly, I couldn't take the exposure.

JOANNE stands.

JOANNE: Would you?

RICKY: What?

JOANNE: Get married one day.

RICKY: Are you pissed?

JOANNE: Why? Does that sound completely ridiculous to you?

RICKY: No, not completely. I mean, I could do the disco, we'd save a fortune.

JOANNE: Change my name.

RICKY: What's wrong with Joanne?

JOANNE: 'Joanne Hill.' Got a ring to it. Be a good day. Be a laugh.

RICKY: Don't think your family would be laughing.

Beat.

Just me, you and Kel then?

36

He bends down, looks at her and holds out his hand.

I'll get the invites printed.

JOANNE: You asking me to marry you?

RICKY: No, I'm asking you to shut up and pass me that wire.

She does so. He tapes over some wires on the floor.

RICHARD enters. He is dripping wet. He stays a good distance away from RICKY and JOANNE, who don't notice him. He seems very uncomfortable and agitated.

Imagine me asking your dad for his blessing.

Beat.

RICKY stands.

Need more tape. I spend half my life running out. When you gonna get me that gaffa tape from work?

JOANNE: I keep forgetting.

RICKY: I had noticed. I'll ask at the bar.

RICKY walks away carrying a PA lead and exits.

RICHARD makes sure RICKY is out of sight before looking over to JOANNE. He wanders over. He has a rucksack on his back and holds a plastic bag which is clearly full. He seems extremely uncomfortable and hovers in front of JOANNE, keeping a safe distance whilst looking at the music gear.

JOANNE: You all right there, love?

RICHARD: Hiya.

JOANNE: Hiya. You all right?

RICHARD: Are you part of the act?

JOANNE: Nah. Just looking after the gear.

RICHARD: Like a roadie are you?

JOANNE: Not exactly.

RICHARD: No. You don't look like a typical roadie.

JOANNE: That's a relief.

Beat.

RICHARD: You haven't got long hair.

JOANNE: …Well…I have!

RICHARD: Oh yeah but you're not a man. With long hair.

Beat.

You're *not* a man, are you?

JOANNE: You what?

RICHARD: No it's just that… Often can't tell. Get it a lot in Amsterdam.

JOANNE: Yeah. Did you wanna put your name down for the karaoke?

RICHARD: Can I sing?

JOANNE: I don't know, can you!? Here y'are, here's the list.

RICHARD: Oh. Thanks.

JOANNE: Know Hayley's family do you? Sid's grand-daughter. The one we're raising money for tonight.

RICHARD: Oh, yeah…sort of.

Beat.

Here. Could I have four-seven-eight?

JOANNE writes down the number.

JOANNE: Four-seven-eight. What's your name?

RICHARD: (*Hesitates, gulps.*) Little Richard.

JOANNE: Right…

JOANNE doesn't write anything.

I'll pass this to Ricky then.

Beat.

RICHARD: D'ya wanna bite of me Chomp?

JOANNE: No ta.

Beat.

RICHARD: This gear, it's all his, is it?

JOANNE: Just the gong.

RICHARD gets a bottle of wine from his rucksack.

RICHARD: Could you give him this?

JOANNE: What for?

RICHARD: There's a raffle on isn't there? As a prize.

JOANNE: Think they've got all the prizes sorted by now.

RICHARD: Right. Well you and Ricky could have it then?

JOANNE: Don't be daft. Do you want me to get Sid?

RICHARD: No, it's... No. Could I just leave it here? I might be going in a bit.

JOANNE: What about your song then?

RICHARD: I'll...I'll see if I'm about. Sorry. Thanks.

RICHARD walks back to his previous spot. He has left his plastic bag. JOANNE examines the wine. RICKY re-enters chewing, holding a pork pie in a napkin.

RICKY: Got ya a pork pie. My God, you *are* on a mission.

JOANNE: Some fella just give me it.

RICKY: Oh aye? Quick mover.

JOANNE: He wanted me to give it to you.

RICKY: Me?

RICKY looks around.

A man?

JOANNE: Black fella. Bit of an 'ead the ball, like. Told him you weren't doing the raffle but he wouldn't listen. And we've got our first singer. That was him as well.

RICKY reads the paper on the karaoke file.

Have you got that one?

RICKY: It's *my* song.

JOANNE: Honest!? No one's ever picked that have they?

RICKY: D'ya think it's a fan?

JOANNE: Must be.

RICKY: Oh great. Tonight of all nights. Why do I always get cranks?

JOANNE: There he is there!

They look over to RICHARD, who has his back to them. RICKY and JOANNE laugh slightly.

RICKY: Bloody ell. It's not a music executive from London then?

JOANNE: Doesn't smell like one!

They laugh.

RICKY: I'm sure he's shaking, look at him!

JOANNE: You wanna hear him speak.

Beat.

Oh let's not stare in case he sees us, he's freakin me out.

RICKY: Why's he rooted to the spot, is he gonna start beggin in a minute or something!?

JOANNE: *(Really suppressing a laugh.)* Oh Ricky don't, it's cruel!

RICKY unfolds the napkin and holds it along his arm. He taps JOANNE.

RICKY: Like to buy a Big Tissue?

JOANNE covers her mouth and laughs hard. RICHARD exits.

Oh he's off.

JOANNE: Ah, shame.

RICKY: What's that there?

JOANNE: Oh. That's his bag, he's gone and left it.

RICKY: Has he definitely gone?

JOANNE: Dunno. Can't see him. Say something over the mic, Rick.

RICKY: I'll do it later, I'm gonna start now.

JOANNE: I'll have a quick root.

RICKY: Jo don't, leave it!

RICKY switches on his mic. JOANNE bends over to the bag.

(Over the mic.) Okay everybody, welcome back. Can we have the lights down please love?

The stage lighting changes.

(Over the mic.) Thanks.

(To JOANNE.) Move to the side Jo, I'm on!

RICKY presses play. A backing track to 'Break My Stride' by Matthew Wilder begins.

(Over the mic.) Time to get things started now then folks. A few eighties memories to kick off the evening.

Cheap graphics appear on RICKY's little karaoke monitor: disco balls, LET'S SING!, IT'S PARTY TIME, fireworks etc.

JOANNE: Jesus Christ!

RICHARD re-enters but neither RICKY nor JOANNE notices.

RICKY: (*To JOANNE.*) What is it?

JOANNE: I dunno! It looks like a dead…ugh, I dunno.

RICKY: (*To JOANNE.*) Well get rid of it, I've started!

RICHARD moves close to them.

RICHARD: Sorry.

RICKY and JOANNE jump and turn to face RICHARD. RICKY is still.

Pause.

The lyrics to the song appear on the screen – RICKY has missed his cue.

The sound of feedback.

I left my bag. I'd forget my head if…erm…you know.

RICHARD walks over to them and picks two sausages out of the bag.

Would either of you like a sausage?

RICHARD and RICKY stare at each other for a long time.

The lights go down and the scene ends but the monitor stays on, and each word colours in time where the singing should be, as the song's backing track plays into…

SCENE FOUR

Saturday (two days later). 3 am. Living room.

RICHARD is on the living room couch under a sleeping bag. JOANNE is standing over him, bladdered. She is wearing her work top, holding a huge kebab and a telephone in its box.

JOANNE: Aah. Look at your little bed. You can't be staying here you know, Richard.

RICHARD: It's fine.

JOANNE: No way. Spare room up there. Be perfect. Soon as 'orror gob clears all that stuff out.

RICHARD: I don't want to mess him about.

JOANNE: You're *my* guest too. I'll look after ya mate. Here y'are shove up.

RICHARD moves up and JOANNE plonks herself next to him.

You had tea tonight?

RICHARD: Had some Coco Pops.

JOANNE: Again? I told Ricky to make sure you ate, haven't seen you have a proper scran yet.

RICHARD: I don't eat much.

JOANNE: Well you do when I'm in charge. Open your mouth.

RICHARD: Wha'?

RICHARD's mouth stays open from 'Wha'?' and JOANNE forces a huge amount of kebab in.

JOANNE: Hope you like chilli sauce.

RICHARD suddenly realises how hot it is.

If anyone's calling the shots here, it's me, d'ya know what I mean? Just remember that.

RICHARD: Is this your house then?

JOANNE: Yeah.

RICHARD: You own it?

JOANNE shrugs.

JOANNE: It's me mum and dad's old house. Jesus Christ that sauce's got arse!

Beat.

Don't worry, they're miles away. Live in Formby now, or Freshfield or whatever it's called.

RICHARD: Have they ever met Ricky?

She laughs more.

JOANNE: God.

She laughs more.

RICHARD: Don't they like him?

Beat.

JOANNE: Our Neil, me brother, he's got a daughter. Called April. It's her birthday next week actually. I'll have to text her…

Beat.

Me dad'd babysit her some Saturdays. She'd always, *always* do her homework on that table, that one there. Dead bright kid, proper sound, bit like Kelisha. I'd help her when I was getting ready to go out. Me dad'd keep goin on about a poster of Will Smith she had on her maths book. He'd call him 'Smigger The Nigger'. All the time, whenever he was on the telly. And d'ya know what he did one night? When she was out the room? He got her Tippex. And got the book. And he coloured his face in.

Beat.

Laughed his head off when she found it.

Pause.

What's a nine-year-old gonna make of that?

Pause.

They have met him actually. Ricky. He did my twenny-first. That's when I first spoke to him.

Beat.

My dad gave him sixty quid.

Beat.

RICHARD: So your mum and dad are grandparents then?

JOANNE: Oh yeah. Proud as punch.

RICHARD: What about you and Ricky then?

JOANNE scoffs.

He's not…*given* you kids then?

Beat.

Not want them…do ya?

JOANNE chews, wipes her hands.

JOANNE: To be honest Rich, and like, I can tell you this cos you're sound and all that, can't I? But me and Ricky, we don't even…

Beat.

So how can we think about kids?

Beat.

I'm like a mum for Kelisha anyway. I'd do anything for her.

RICHARD: You're not that much older than her though really, are you?

JOANNE: Yeah but…I still try me best. I'm a good *mate* for her. Jeez me mouth's burning here.

She notices a photo frame on a table.

Ah, there she is! Little Kel.

Beat.

Funny looking baby though wasn't she? Baldy 'ead. Ricky teases her by saying he used to call her Kelisha Alopecia! Big clumps of tatty hair.

RICHARD's face has suddenly turned sour.

Bless her. It's so good to see her growing up now you know. I'm so proud of her, she works so hard at her studyin –

RICHARD: No.

JOANNE: What?

RICHARD: That wasn't his joke. It was mine, I'd say it. Kelisha Alopecia.

JOANNE: Yeah. Okay Rich.

RICHARD: He doesn't still call her that now does he?

JOANNE: No.

Beat.

She's got plenty of hair now.

Beat.

She loves the bones of *you* doesn't she? These past few days.

Beat.

Good on her. I reckon you'll do her the world of good, Rich. Get her out of her shell. You could do it. Bit of a change for her. I get on with her great and all that but…feels like the other day *I* was her age. Look at me now.

She backhands the kebab.

This is the highlight of my week.

Beat.

I'm thirty this year.

Beat.

RICHARD: We should have a party.

Beat.

JOANNE: You know all these people you see at work every day.
When you're on your knees cleaning a bottom shelf. And they
look down at ya like you're something they might step in. And
you move out their way and don't even get a thanks. And you
recognise some of them from when you were a kid, and you
know they've clocked ya and thought... 'Look at you now'.
But you always think, 'Fine. So what. You're the low-arse
who'll always keep coming here. I'll be gone soon.'

Beat.

But then ten years pass and you realise you won't, unless you
do something.

Beat.

I'd just love to have the chance to...start all over again, you
know? With new people. D'ya ever get that? Or do something
else. Does that make me bad? I've *always* wanted to though.
And there was a time I thought I *would.* With Ricky. *Still*
would. Still *waitin.*

Beat.

RICHARD: What you waiting for?

JOANNE: I dunno.

*A toilet flush is heard off. An upstairs light comes on. RICHARD
and JOANNE look up.*

Beat.

RICHARD: Get paid to join the mile high club.

JOANNE: What?

RICHARD: Look, in here. This is the free mag I got off the plane
the other day. 'Get paid to join the mile high club – cabin
crew wanted now.'

JOANNE: Whereabouts?

RICHARD: Look, all that page.

JOANNE: No, where's the work based?

RICHARD: On the plane.

JOANNE: (*Reading.*) Stansted. (*To RICHARD, 'end of conversation'.*)
London.

RICHARD: Is that a problem? Who says you have to work in
Liverpool?

Beat.

You should do it.

Beat.

Here you are, it says what you need to be.

JOANNE eats her kebab.

(*Reading.*) 'Aged eighteen or over.'

JOANNE: Yay!

RICHARD: (*Reading.*) 'Six months' face-to-face customer service
experience.'

JOANNE: Yay!

RICHARD: (*Reading.*) 'Friendly and personable.'

JOANNE does a vulgar smile, food in her mouth.

(*Reading.*) 'A good listener.'

JOANNE: What?

RICHARD: (*Reading.*) 'A good listener.'

JOANNE: What?

RICHARD: A good…

Beat.

(*Reading.*) 'Able to swim at least twenty-five metres.'

JOANNE: Oh shite, I've lost me certificate.

Beat.

RICHARD: Okay.

RICHARD drops the magazine.

Beat.

I know. It's scary for you, I know.

Beat.

JOANNE: Hang on a minute. Who's scared?

RICHARD: Well…

JOANNE picks up the magazine.

JOANNE: Yeah well. Maybe I'm just tired right now. And I might be able to look at it properly with a clear head.

Beat.

RICHARD: You should keep hold of it.

JOANNE: I will.

The upstairs light goes off.

Beat.

So anyway. Richard. Little Richard. Why did ya go?

RICHARD: What?

JOANNE: All those years ago.

Beat.

RICHARD: What does Ricky say?

JOANNE: Why did you leave?

RICHARD: It's all…long time ago now.

JOANNE: Did you leave before or after Miranda?

Beat.

When she left the baby.

JOANNE leans in and whispers.

Were you there for all that? Cos yous musta been close being in the band together ey?

RICHARD is motionless yet definitely at breaking point now, staring at JOANNE, who is so drunk and busy eating that she's pretty oblivious.

He's never told me anything.

RICHARD looks down. JOANNE stands.

Ugh, I've gotta get a drink. You want anything? Oh here y'are. This is Sid's old phone. Said we can have it.

She takes it out and plugs it in.

RICHARD: Does it work?

JOANNE: Only one way to find out.

She dials her mobile. The phone rings. JOANNE laughs. RICHARD sits up concerned.

RICHARD: Won't we wake the others?

The answer phone kicks in. Sid's warm Scouse voice: 'Allo. This is Sid. I'm either out, or I can't be arsed answering. Leave a message.' JOANNE is amused. She hands RICHARD her mobile.

JOANNE: (*Impersonating Sid.*) 'Leave a message.'

JOANNE exits. RICHARD sits for a moment, helpless.

RICHARD: One-two. Hello. It's Richard. Little Richard. Not sure what I should say. I'm on my own. Everyone else is…somewhere else.

RICKY enters.

RICHARD looks closely at the new phone.

I think everything is looking okay. I hope so anyway. It will be as long as you're listening to this. Peace and love. Bye.

JOANNE enters with a glass of water.

JOANNE: (*To RICKY.*) What *you* doing up!?

RICKY: Why's the phone goin?

JOANNE: Got us a new one. Sick of waitin for you. Good ey?

RICHARD: Sorry if I woke you, Rick.

RICKY: That's okay.

JOANNE: D'ya wanna bevvy?

KELISHA enters.

Yay! Here she is! Let's have a little party!

KELISHA: Ha ha!

JOANNE: What?

KELISHA: You're rotten!

JOANNE: I am not! I haven't touched a cunt dropstable.

RICKY: Joanne.

Beat.

Come on, Kel.

JOANNE: Ah ey! You leaving?

RICKY: You in in the morning?

JOANNE: Well yeah, but not till ten. Have you chased up any of
those numbers from the club yet?

RICKY: Haven't had time.

JOANNE: Now is the time Ricky!

RICKY: What, three in the morning?

JOANNE: It's not three o'clock. Is it?

Beat.

RICKY: See ya up there.

KELISHA: Y'all right Rich?

RICHARD: Y'all right Kel?

KELISHA: Do you sleep in your socks!?

RICHARD: Yeah.

KELISHA: Just like me, I do too! These two skit me!

RICHARD and KELISHA smile together.

Night.

RICKY and KELISHA exit.

JOANNE: Night Kel.

Pause.

(*Finds it touching.*) Aaah.

Beat.

Am I keeping you up mate?

RICHARD gets on his back again.

RICHARD: Not at all.

JOANNE: Here y'are. Sort this pillow out. You taking your hat off?

*JOANNE removes his hat. He has a huge scar and clumps of his hair
are missing. JOANNE laughs.*

Pause.

You lie down, that's it. You comfy?

RICHARD: Mm. Thank you.

JOANNE: Right then. Come here.

JOANNE sits on the edge of the sofa and gives him a hug and a squeeze.

Sleep tight mate.

RICHARD: G'night.

JOANNE: And you know. We've had a good little chat haven't we? Let's just…between me and you, ey? To ourselves for now. Yeah?

RICHARD: Yeah.

JOANNE: Promise?

RICHARD: Promise.

JOANNE: Good. What's that there?

She points to his chest, he looks down. She runs her finger up to his face and laughs. She grabs his face and kisses him on the lips. She stands, picks up the kebab paper, scrunches it up again, holds it, then stands still. She sighs a heavy sigh.

I really don't wanna go to bed.

JOANNE stares up at the ceiling, sighs again, then exits to the stairs, walking heavily, knocking the light off.

RICHARD is on his back, eyes open, staring up, dead still. He picks up the photo frame and examines it.

The living room door opens slightly. RICKY stands in the doorway.

RICKY: You warm enough?

RICHARD drops the frame and sits up.

RICHARD: Ricky.

RICKY: Got another blanket here for you, if you want it.

RICHARD: Oh no. Honestly, no need. Bag's dead warm.

RICKY: Sure?

RICHARD: Yeah.

Beat.

Thanks anyway.

Beat.

RICKY: Okay then.

Beat.

RICHARD: Okay Rick.

RICKY goes to shut the door.

Can you leave the light on?

Beat.

RICKY: Still prefer it that way ey?

RICHARD: Yeah. Did I…used to…did I?

RICKY: We both did.

Beat.

RICHARD: Do *you* still?

RICKY: No.

Beat.

RICKY knocks the light on.

RICHARD: Thanks bruv.

Beat.

Night then.

The sound of a fast train approaching a platform fades up.

RICKY: Night Richard.

The train gets louder and its horn blows into…

SCENE FIVE

Thursday (five days later). 6.30 am. Train station platform.

KELISHA and RICHARD are sat on a bench, reading a brochure. JOANNE is standing looking anxiously at the train, holding a bottle of Pepsi.

KELISHA: (*Reading.*) 'Some universities have about as much credibility as your dad dancing at a wedding. But not this one.'

JOANNE: Why aren't the doors open yet?

RICHARD: Your dad's *sung* at weddings, tell them that.

KELISHA: Ey yeah!

They smile together.

JOANNE: It's the first train, it shouldn't need cleaning.

KELISHA: Jo, help me out! What can I say that'll impress them?

JOANNE swigs from her Pepsi.

RICHARD: (*Loudly.*) Lipsmackin-thirstquenchin-acetastin-
motivatin-cooltalkin-highwalkin-fastlivin-evergivin-
coolfizzing...Pepsi!

KELISHA: How d'ya do that!

JOANNE: I can say it, by the way.

KELISHA: Liar.

JOANNE braces herself and says it quietly.

JOANNE: Lipsmackin-thirstquenchin-acetastin-motivatin-
cooltalkin-highwalkin-fastlivin-evergivin-coolfizzing...Pepsi.

KELISHA roars with laughter.

Beat.

God, where is he? I don't even wanna coffee.

RICHARD: Your legs are shaking, Jo.

KELISHA: Shoulda worn your furry boots! Are they new shoes?

JOANNE: No.

KELISHA: You didn't have to dress up all smart for me, you know.
Look at you in your going out gear.

JOANNE: This isn't me going out gear!

KELISHA: It's a university we're going to. Ripped jeans are
probably more appropriate.

JOANNE: Do us a favour Rich, go and see how long Ricky's gonna
be, we should be getting on now.

RICHARD: Right.

RICHARD exits.

JOANNE lights a cigarette.

KELISHA: Jo!

JOANNE tuts and puts the cigarette away.

Come and sit down.

JOANNE sits. KELISHA links her arm.

Beat.

JOANNE: I had ripped jeans. My dad cut them up for me. When I was nine. I was into Wham!. Can do the whole of the Wham Rap.

KELISHA: Ha, you saddo! Go on then. Rap for me.

JOANNE: Sod off.

KELISHA: Can't remember it?

JOANNE: Know every word.

KELISHA: Prove it! Bottler.

Beat.

Hey Jo. Was thinking. We could get something when we arrive. Brochure says there's a café on the campus, look. Looks all right, dunnit?

KELISHA looks at the brochure. JOANNE doesn't.

JOANNE: Listen Kel.

KELISHA: Size of the place!

JOANNE: This is gonna sound a bit mad but…

Beat.

There's a reason I booked this train for today.

KELISHA: Cos the tickets were cheaper.

JOANNE: I wish. I booked them…

Beat.

KELISHA: What Jo?

JOANNE: I booked…after I'd made another call.

KELISHA: Right.

Beat.

JOANNE: EasyJet.

Beat.

I've got a…an interview. For a…job. Today. Stansted.

KELISHA: Air hostess?

JOANNE: Flight attendant, please. I…saw an advert.

KELISHA: Where is that?

JOANNE: It's down by –

KELISHA: London. You're going…to London, now.

Beat.

But that's not where the job'll be. Is it?

JOANNE: Well, no. I hope. Well maybe at first. Not sure yet. It's a recruitment week. They said pick your day. So I did. Today's the only day I can get off, got no holidays left.

Beat.

I won't…like. Not if you need me to come with you.

KELISHA: So my dad doesn't know?

Beat.

God Jo! If you'd have told me this earlier I wouldn't have had to go today!

JOANNE: You *wanna* go though don't ya?

KELISHA: Yeah but not on me own!

JOANNE: Oh, fine. *Fine.* I'm sorry. In fact ya dad can have my ticket.

KELISHA: NO! I don't want him there, I wanna show him I can do it, that's the whole point!

JOANNE looks shocked. She grabs for a cigarette.

JOANNE: Ah I'm definitely havin a fag now.

Beat.

So…you think it's a stupid idea goin for this?

KELISHA: Me? (*Turning away.*) Not really my concern is it.

JOANNE: Course it is Kel.

KELISHA: Why can't you just look for a normal job, what's so great about this? Don't you think my interview's a bit more important, it's my whole future!

JOANNE: I know it is! But what about mine?

Beat.

Who d'ya think's gonna pay for all this?

She pokes KELISHA's university brochure.

KELISHA: *I* will!

JOANNE: Well it's gonna be hard Kel. I wanna make sure you can do it…you're my girl.

Beat.

Look, I'm sorry if it's upset ya. Come here.

JOANNE puts her arm round KELISHA, who doesn't respond.

Beat.

I shoulda told ya, I know. I've been worried sick all week. I know this is your big day, I just thought…oh here they are! Right. Listen. Kel…let's just not say anything to your dad for now, ey? Okay?

Beat.

Kelisha will you speak to me!?

Beat.

We'll talk about it on the train. It'll be fine.

RICKY and RICHARD enter, carrying four coffees.

KELISHA: So will I be getting the train back on me own?

JOANNE: Ssh.

RICHARD: Hey hey hey ladies! Four coffees! Who's for sugar?

RICHARD uses both hands to pull out a ridiculous number of sugar sachets from his side pockets, brown in one, white in the other.

White or brown?

JOANNE: No ta, listen, we're gonna have to shoot.

RICKY: It's not time.

JOANNE: People are getting on. How much was all that?

RICKY: Seven pounds and ninety-six pence.

JOANNE: I'll give you some money.

RICKY: I don't need money.

RICHARD: Seen this, Jo?

RICHARD gets a crumpled magazine article from his pocket and shows it to JOANNE.

JOANNE: Oh my God. Don't think you ever showed me that one, Rick!

RICHARD: That's me on the left.

JOANNE: You look so…different.

RICHARD: I used to love my hair.

JOANNE: Have you got eyeliner on there, Ricky?

RICKY: No.

JOANNE: You bloody have.

KELISHA: Look at that bit in the interview there. 'The Brothers Hill are inseparable, finishing each other's sentences, mucking about like schoolboys during the photo shoot.'

RICHARD: Where was it taken, Rick?

RICKY: Mum's. Backyard.

KELISHA: Haven't you got a copy?

RICKY: Might have. Packed away somewhere. You gonna be warm enough?

KELISHA: Yep.

RICHARD: D'ya wanna borrow my hat?

KELISHA: No ta.

JOANNE: Hey, talking of hats, are we still on for Sid's sixtieth tomorrow night or what? It's a hat party.

KELISHA: Not in a pub is it?

JOANNE: No, just in his house. Okay everyone? Right, let's go.

KELISHA: See ya Rich, see ya Dad.

RICKY: See ya. Be good.

KELISHA: What yous doing now?

RICKY: Nothing. Get the bus back.

JOANNE: (*Walking off.*) Let Richard shift all that heavy stuff out the spare room.

Train whistle.

Come on Kel.

JOANNE and KELISHA hurry off.

KELISHA: (*Off.*) See ya!

RICKY and RICHARD watch them board the train. They make the odd wave at the same time.

RICHARD: Y'all right Rick?

Beat.

I'm lovin this! It's been good seeing each other again. Been a long time. Too long. I'm lovin it.

Beat.

It's great that I can stay with you for the long term. Get to know each other again.

RICKY: Long term?

RICHARD: Yeah.

RICKY: What does that mean?

RICHARD: It's what Joanne said at the weekend. She was just being friendly.

RICKY: She was just being bladdered.

RICHARD: Was she wrong then?

Beat.

I could go and stay with Uncle James.

RICKY: He's moved.

RICHARD: Where to?

RICKY: Bell Road.

RICHARD: Where?

RICKY: You know the crematorium?

RICHARD: Yeah.

Pause.

He's there? *Underneath?* God, how come I didn't know? Bet he was disappointed I wasn't there.

RICKY: Yeah.

RICHARD: Did he say that?

RICKY: Not on the day.

Beat.

RICHARD: It is Joanne's house though, isn't it?

RICKY: Oh you wanna play it like that do ya?

RICHARD: No.

Beat.

She's nice, Joanne. I like her.

Beat.

I never knew you went out with white girls.

RICKY: What's that supposed to mean?

RICHARD: You know. When we were younger. I thought you always used to go with just black girls. Didn't you?

RICKY: How the hell would you know?

RICHARD: I'm sure of it…you used to.

RICKY: And what makes you think I don't now?

RICHARD: What?

RICKY: What makes you think I don't now?

RICHARD: You mean…you see other girls too?

RICKY: No.

RICHARD: Just Joanne?

RICKY: Yeah.

RICHARD: She's white though.

RICKY: Says who?

Beat.

RICHARD: Joanne?

Beat.

She's black?

Beat.

Oh. I thought she was white.

Beat.

She looks…like she could be white.

RICKY: So what?

RICHARD: Oh. Yeah. She's mixed race then?

Beat.

Yeah. Course.

Beat.

Ricky?

RICKY looks up at a screen.

RICKY: Where's this train ending up?

Beat.

RICHARD: Not sure.

Beat.

Why?

RICKY looks around for signs.

RICKY: London.

Beat.

RICHARD: Yeah. London.

Beat.

The Big Smoke.

The sound of the train leaving.

They're leaving. It's going.

Beat.

D'ya remember us getting the train back from London, Ricky?

Beat.

Hey?

RICHARD walks over to him, puts his arm on his shoulder.

Ricky?

RICKY: Where's the…?

RICKY looks at RICHARD, then back at the train.

RICHARD: Can you remember? We got the train didn't we? And
I was drunk? Remember that DJ with the beard? He had a
nickname. He loved me. It was his fault me getting drunk. He
took me drinking.

Beat.

He took me. And Miranda. Where were you? You went
working somewhere.

Beat.

RICKY sits on the bench, his back and RICHARD giving him pain.

You okay? Is your back all right?

Beat.

Always working. Always having those meetings. Never stopped. Did you? Obsessed!

RICHARD joins RICKY on the bench, sits close to him, faces him, trying to get RICKY to respond.

What was his name? The DJ. Something something... something? He said our name and we played on the telly. It was amazing. We watched it back home. In Mum's. Didn't we mate? With Miranda. And the baby.

Beat.

It was the best thing we ever did, down in London, on the telly, you know! TOP OF THE POPS! It was *Top of the Pops!* Wasn't it!? It was insane! Insane Ricky! All the lights and the... *smoke...* glitter stuff in the air... big *balloons.* Everyone had hold of balloons right next to us, apart from me and you, dancing by us, cheering all through, clapping at the start! It was chocker blocker, all strangers on the stage, I couldn't even *see* you! I fell over! We were only miming, we didn't stop laughing. And you said your hairs stood up at the end. You must have had hair then. Do you remember Ricky? Your long hair. Hairy! That was him! The presenter! The Hairy Man or something. He had a laugh with me. Said I was dead funny. He musta liked you too, but he really took a shine to me.

Beat.

He said our name and we played on the telly.

Beat. RICKY is staring at the train.

Ricky?

RICKY: WHAT!?

Pause.

I don't know what you're talking about.

Pause.

RICHARD: It did happen though. I know it did.

Beat.

Why are you still here Ricky?

Beat.

You always said we'd end up there.

Beat.

I know *I* haven't. I didn't know if I'd ever see you again. But I always thought you'd be living it up in London by now.

Beat.

RICKY: What exactly do you remember, Richard?

Beat.

RICHARD: Are you getting angry with me?

RICKY: Just answer the question. You know, whatever this 'thing' is you've got, I'm just not quite sure what it means. Have you got short term or long term or selective loss, have you been pumped full of drugs, are you a little bit simple now, are you just full of shit...

RICKY suddenly squeezes the polystyrene container in RICHARD's hand and the hot coffee spills onto them. RICHARD quietly cries out in pain, holding his hand. RICKY holds his own hand.

I'm sorry. Richard, I'm –

RICHARD moves away slightly. The two men hold their hands, faces anguished.

The echoey station noises – tannoy, trolleys, chatter, machinery – all get louder.

The Electric Hills song fades up with crowd noise. It is an instrumental section and plays for a few short bars before jolting to a stop, the last note echoing and reverbing into the silence.

End of Act One.

ACT TWO

FM radio static. The Electric Hills song plays, near its end. This time it is a 'clean' version without any crowd noise. Dave Lee Travis speaks over the end of the song and we realise we are listening to Radio 1 from 1988. He mentions that the song is climbing up the charts and that the boys recorded for tonight's Top of the Pops with him earlier that week. He got on famously with Little Richard and they went drinking together.

An 80s Radio 1 jingle plays.

DLT announces 'it's time to drag up the past with a little something from 18 years ago', and 'Crocodile Rock' by Elton John begins and plays over the audience into...

SCENE SIX

Friday (the next day). 11 pm. Sid's Kitchen.

JOANNE is wearing a yellow hard hat. She is lighting a cigarette. She cheekily wiggles to the music and goes over to KELISHA to top up her glass of wine. KELISHA is wearing a glittery pork-pie hat. We see KELISHA mouthing to JOANNE to stop, covering her glass, she doesn't want any more. JOANNE gives in and necks wine herself.

RICKY enters opening a can of lager, wearing a baseball cap with a ridiculous looking blond pony tail. The music shrinks onto the small ghetto blaster in the kitchen. There is a party going on in the cellar.

KELISHA: Barry White.

JOANNE: Wayne Rooney.

RICKY: Richard Stilgoe.

KELISHA: Simon Cowell.

JOANNE: Colin Farrell.

RICKY: Freddie Starr.

KELISHA: Sean Paul.

RICKY sharply knocks Elton John off.

RICKY: Shurrup ya fat queen.

JOANNE: Oi!

RICKY: Makes me wanna puke.

JOANNE: Maybe he hated your song!

RICKY: Yeah I did too, that was one of his worst ones.

JOANNE: Paul Gascoigne.

RICKY: Gordon Ramsay.

KELISHA: Rik Mayall.

JOANNE: Michael Jackson.

RICKY: Jimmy Saville.

KELISHA: Simon Webbe.

JOANNE: (*To KELISHA.*) Oof.

KELISHA: (*To JOANNE.*) Oof.

RICKY: Get on with it.

JOANNE: Winston Churchill.

RICHARD enters wearing a policeman's helmet.

RICHARD: Does anyone need a drink? Loadsa beers in the fridge down here!

KELISHA: No ta, Rich!

Pause. RICHARD stands, smiles at everyone, then exits quickly.

RICKY: Chuck Berry.

KELISHA: Billie Piper.

JOANNE: Paul McCartney.

RICKY: Michel Platini.

KELISHA: Pete Burns.

JOANNE: Bill Clinton.

RICKY: Chris Rock.

KELISHA: Ricky Hill!

RICKY: No.

JOANNE: Why not?

RICKY: Famous.

KELISHA: You are famous!

RICKY: Properly.

KELISHA: You are properly famous!

RICKY: Come on, R.

JOANNE: She's done R!

KELISHA: H, Jo.

RICKY: No.

KELISHA: Yes.

RICKY: Say someone famous.

KELISHA: I've said you!

RICKY: Well you can't *have* me! Stop being stupid! We play properly or not at all.

Beat.

Laughter from outside.

KELISHA: Rick...James.

Beat. JOANNE is looking towards the cellar.

Jo?

JOANNE: Sorry love, what am I on?

KELISHA: J.

JOANNE: Erm...Ken Dodd.

KELISHA: No not K – J!

JOANNE: Oh, Jerry Springer.

RICKY: Ken Dodd invented this game, you know?

KELISHA: Did he?

RICKY: No, Doddy.

RICHARD enters wearing an incredibly huge afro.

RICHARD: Ricky! Come down, some of the boys – they want us to sing!

RICKY: Maybe later.

JOANNE: Go on Ricky, you and Richard do a turn, I'll get Sid to gather everyone.

RICKY: A *turn*? What am I, Arthur Askey?

JOANNE: Misery arse.

KELISHA: Who's Arthur Askey?

JOANNE: He went to school with your dad.

RICKY: Pass us a fork please, Kel.

RICHARD: I don't remember an Arthur Askey in our school.

KELISHA: You eatin again!?

Somebody shouts for RICHARD in the other room. RICHARD exits.

RICKY: Sheena Easton.

KELISHA: Er…Elton…Elton…

KELISHA gestures to the ghetto blaster, the name escapes her.

JOANNE: Come on, you can only say 'Welsby' or 'John', how many Eltons do you know!?

KELISHA: John! I forgot his name, Elton John.

RICKY: Fat queen!

JOANNE: Kelisha, get yourself a drink.

KELISHA: I will in a bit, Elton John.

RICKY: Fat queen!

JOANNE: Will you stop saying that!

RICKY: Can't you smoke outside?

JOANNE: It's a *party*.

KELISHA: Hurry up, Jo!

JOANNE: Erm…what am I on again?

KELISHA: J! Elton John!

RICKY: Fat queen!

JOANNE: Shut up!

RICKY: Hurry up then!

JOANNE: Johnny Depp!

RICKY: Are you just naming fellas you fancy?

JOANNE: No!

KELISHA: Come on Dad. D.

JOANNE: I said Wayne Rooney before, who the hell fancies him?

RICKY: David Blunkett.

JOANNE: Well he might!

They all laugh.

KELISHA: Barbara Windsor.

JOANNE: Warren Beatty.

Beat.

RICKY: Is it me?

JOANNE/KELISHA: Yes!

RICKY: B…erm…

RICKY does an awful Bruce Forsyth impression.

JOANNE: The friggin ell was that?

RICKY: Brucie.

JOANNE: Has he had a stroke or something?

KELISHA: It's a repeat, need another B.

RICKY: Erm…

JOANNE: Quickly.

RICKY: B, B.

JOANNE: Three.

RICKY: Hang on!

JOANNE/KELISHA: Two!

RICKY: Er…

JOANNE/KELISHA: One!

RICKY: Bungle off Rainbow!

JOANNE: Too late!

RICKY: I got it!

KELISHA: Ooh just.

JOANNE: He's not having that! Drink this.

RICKY: No chance!

KELISHA: What is it?

JOANNE: It's good stuff, it's Jose Cuervo.

RICKY: No way, Jose.

KELISHA: You're drinking even less than me, Dad!

RICKY: I can't have shots, they make me feel funny.

JOANNE: Fat queen!

KELISHA: I'm still knackered from yesterday. Musta walked round the whole campus twice!

JOANNE: Get on the sauce then, soon sort ya.

RICKY: Aren't you knackered, Jo?

JOANNE: Ey?

RICKY: From yesterday, with Kel?

JOANNE: Oh…nah, obviously just fitter than you Kel, ey?

Beat.

JOANNE grabs some gaffer tape.

Oh yeah, have you seen this present for ya?

RICKY: Gaffer tape. At last.

JOANNE: Sid brought it home from work today cos he knew you were coming!

RICKY: A month I've been waiting for that.

KELISHA: Might get some peace now!

Beat.

JOANNE: Why don't we go down?

KELISHA: I'd rather stay here I reckon.

JOANNE: Some of Sid's grandkids are a bit tasty, get in there.

RICKY: Our Kel's too classy for those divvies.

JOANNE: Look like nice lads. That little one in the tight t-shirt, Kel? Dead brown.

RICKY: Dead orange more like. Does he work in the chocolate factory?

JOANNE: He mightn't be tall but he's broad, he looks like he's been training.

RICKY: He looks like he's been Tangoed, the little fanny.

JOANNE: He'd have you.

RICKY: I bet he would.

JOANNE: Come on then, let's get some music going.

KELISHA: I'll do another drink for Rich. What you sticking on Jo?

JOANNE: One of those free ones out the paper.

KELISHA: Let's have a look.

'My Sharona' by The Knack begins.

JOANNE: *Come* on!

JOANNE claps along and tries to get KELISHA to dance. RICKY eats chilli from a pan. RICHARD enters wearing a cowboy hat with a comedy axe attached. He heads for the middle of the kitchen to dance. His dance is a bizarre mixture of bodypopping, moonwalking and a Max Wall strut. JOANNE and KELISHA clap along.

RICHARD grabs KELISHA and they hold each other with both hands, facing each other, dancing round, Ring-a-ring-o'-roses style, joyous.

RICHARD stops, worn out, and JOANNE searches for a new song.

Woohoo! Love it Rich!

RICHARD: Oof! Can't remember the last time I danced like that.

RICKY: I can't remember the last time anyone danced like that.

JOANNE: What's that your drinking, Rich?

RICHARD: Lager and Fanta.

KELISHA: Together?

RICKY: At last.

KELISHA: Will ya come the toilet with me Jo?

RICKY: Are you gonna be sick?

KELISHA: Course not! There's no lock on the door.

JOANNE: Okay, just finish this ciggy.

RICHARD: I'll take you.

RICKY: I'll go.

RICHARD: You finish your food.

RICKY: I have.

Beat.

RICKY and KELISHA exit.

JOANNE: Come on mate, shall we get some more tunes going?

JOANNE searches through the CDs.

RICHARD: Went well yesterday then?

JOANNE stops and looks at RICHARD.

Kelisha said.

Beat.

JOANNE: God, she doesn't half confide in you doesn't she?

Beat.

Can't blame her I suppose.

Beat.

Ah Richard. Just praying they ask me back. I mean, I reckon they will? Unless they're like that with everyone.

RICHARD: No! They'll have seen how good you are.

JOANNE: Had to do all this 'roleplay'. I was *that* close to leaving. In fact I tried. Pretended I needed the toilet. But the main door was locked. Went back in and there was this game started. Had to 'appease an irate customer'. The interviewer played him. Me nerves were shot. Wanted to run away. But d'ya know what? Out of ten of us, I was the only one who made him back down. He said to me after, I had a look in my eye.

Beat.

I was just…petrified. Actually *shaking.* Scared of it all. Like you said I was. I thought of you. And then I thought 'why am I?' Which got me upset. *Angry.* But when we'd finished, when he shook me hand and I was asked back…I felt like huggin him to death.

RICHARD: You shoulda done!

JOANNE smiles, goes back to searching the CDs.

Hey Jo. You'll be able to buy yourself a decent car!

JOANNE: Oh God yeah, too right.

RICHARD: What will you buy?

JOANNE: Dunno. Torn between a red Ferrari and a white Lamborghini.

RICHARD: Really?

JOANNE: Don't be daft!

RICHARD: Oh right!

Beat.

Actually, if the police ever saw *you* driving one of them, they'd just be constantly pulling you over wouldn't they?

JOANNE: Why?

RICHARD: Well, you know. With you being black.

Beat.

JOANNE: Ey?

RICHARD: You know what the bizzies are like.

JOANNE: What do you mean with me being black?

RICHARD: Well…you are. Aren't you?

JOANNE: No.

RICHARD: Right.

JOANNE: Why did you think that?

RICHARD: I thought Ricky…sorry. I'm just a bit pissed, I suppose.

JOANNE: Ricky said that to you?

RICHARD: Yeah.

JOANNE: He obviously thinks everything's a big joke.

RICHARD: S'pose he doesn't mean no harm.

JOANNE: Well he should know better than tormenting you over something like that.

RICHARD: I'm sorry Joanne.

Beat.

I just see you as…a really beautiful woman.

JOANNE: My God you are pissed. But so am I, so I'll drink to that!

JOANNE swigs and passes RICHARD her empty glass.

Do us a top up there please, Rich.

RICHARD: Sure. Hey Jo. Do you want the wine *I* got ya? With the token?

JOANNE: Oh aye yeah! Good lad Richie, that'll do me.

RICHARD goes to pour the wine.

Oh my God!

RICHARD freezes.

RICHARD: What?

JOANNE: Richard!

RICHARD: What's wrong?

JOANNE: You're on this CD out the paper! Look! 'The Electric Hills'. I'm sticking it on! Track fourteen.

The fog horn at the beginning of 'Night Boat To Cairo' by Madness plays.

Is this it?

RICHARD: This is Madness.

JOANNE: I know!

RICHARD: No, this isn't us, I think this is Madness.

JOANNE: Oh, next track.

JOANNE selects the next song. JOANNE looks at RICHARD in delight. The CD jumps.

Shit, what's going on there? Must be dirty.

RICKY and KELISHA re-enter.

RICKY: Decided to do a bit of housework or something?

JOANNE: We've found your song!

KELISHA: Honest?

RICHARD: Yeah!

KELISHA: Oh look! It's got in brackets 'written by Hill slash Hill' then 'produced by Captain Flashrock the Third'. Who the hell's that?

RICKY: A sound engineer called Dave. *I* produced it.

JOANNE: Here it is!

The fog horn at the start of 'Night Boat To Cairo' by Madness plays.

RICKY: That's Madness.

JOANNE: What? Oh, next track.

The song plays again. And freezes at the exactly the same point as earlier.

Aagh! Bastard CD player!

KELISHA: Ah no, is it scratched bad?

JOANNE: Must be.

RICKY: That's a pity, I've only got about seven hundred copies of it in ours.

KELISHA: Yeah but it would have been so special to play it now.

JOANNE: Never mind. I think it's definitely time for a little toast.

RICKY: I've just eaten, thanks.

JOANNE: Everyone, get your glasses. Ready? Okay. Here's…to us! To the Hills!

JOANNE/KELISHA/RICHARD: The Hills!

They all touch glasses.

KELISHA: What else is there to put on, Jo?

JOANNE: Come and be DJ.

KELISHA and JOANNE go through the CDs.

RICHARD: Havin a good time Rick?

RICKY: Whale.

JOANNE: Get us a drink, Kel.

KELISHA: Hang on Jo, Jesus!

RICKY: Kelisha. Language.

JOANNE tuts.

JOANNE: Have you picked something?

KELISHA: Yeah, here y'are.

KELISHA presses play and 'Please Don't Go' by KC and the Sunshine Band begins. JOANNE mimes the 'I love you' to KELISHA and forces her into a slowie, the two of them laughing.

RICHARD: So Joanne, when's the next interview?

JOANNE stops.

JOANNE: Oh you mean…me advert? I was just telling Richard, the local paper wants to interview us about…our work's advert on the telly.

RICHARD: What advert? I was talking…about…the…

JOANNE gestures to RICHARD to stop but even as she does it, realises it's too late, the others are looking. RICHARD withdraws.

Beat.

RICKY lowers the music.

RICKY: Talking about what, Richard?

RICHARD: No, it…

RICHARD shakes his head.

RICKY: Finish your sentence.

Beat.

Have you forgotten? Has your head gone funny again? D'ya wanna clue? Shall we play another game?

RICKY puts his arms out, does an aeroplane.

Pause. RICKY smiles horribly at everyone.

Come on, that's your first clue, easy.

Beat.

You two, you can help. Let's remind him what was he talking ab–

KELISHA: Dad, please, don't…

RICKY: Oh sorry. Can't *I* play this game? Just for you three?

JOANNE: Kelisha! After all we said?

KELISHA: What? I haven't said a word!

JOANNE: You couldn't go five minutes without shooting your mouth off?

KELISHA: Ah no, Jo. Please don't think that!

JOANNE: Well then how did –

RICKY: I found out for myself. They rang to confirm your interview.

KELISHA: Ya see!

RICKY: (*To KELISHA.*) Though I dunno how you can stand there and look me in the eye, you must've known all along what she's been up to! No wonder you didn't want your own dad to go yesterday, not if it would've upset your little scam together. But you're too busy wrapped up in your own stupid pipe dreams to care about my feelings, aren't you?

JOANNE: What do you mean *your* feelings –

RICKY: And don't try and tell me it's just coincidence that you're both pissing off at the same time! Am I so…*unbearable*?

KELISHA: No one's leaving you, Dad!

RICKY: Oh so you're both gonna get the bus home to see me every day are you? One's two-hundred miles away, the other one's twice as far!

JOANNE: Can you blame us!?

RICHARD: I think I'd better go.

JOANNE: I think we've *all* had enough.

RICKY: I know *I* have.

RICHARD: No. I really should leave now. On my own.

KELISHA: We'll all get a cab.

RICHARD: I'm so sorry.

JOANNE: Yeah, well it's not your fault Richard. It's been a long time coming.

RICKY: So what's Richard got that I haven't then ey? That you'd tell *him*?

RICHARD drops his glass which smashes. He bends over to pick up the pieces. KELISHA bends down with him.

KELISHA: Richard!

RICHARD: Ricky.

Beat.

You've got to tell me mate.

KELISHA: Come here Rich.

RICHARD: Please Rick!

RICKY: What?

RICHARD: About when we were last…together. It's killing me! Thing is, I *know*. I mean, I don't, but I've known all this time, since I've seen you.

JOANNE: What's he going on about now?

RICHARD: What did I *do*?

KELISHA: What's he on about, Dad?

RICKY: Ignore him. He's off his face.

RICHARD stops himself, suddenly out of breath. A moment of realisation has just smacked him in the face.

RICHARD: Bye Ricky.

RICHARD rises and heads for the back door, knocking KELISHA off balance. JOANNE grabs him.

KELISHA: Richard!

JOANNE: Where d'ya think you're going, I'll phone us a cab now. And we'll all go together.

RICKY: Let him go!

JOANNE: Calm him down! Ricky!

RICHARD: It's something to do with Miranda isn't it?

RICKY: You WHAT?

RICHARD: I loved her.

RICKY: Shut. Your Mouth. Now.

RICHARD: No, I mean as a kind of –

RICKY suddenly pulls open the gaffer tape and wraps it over RICHARD's mouth and round his head. As the men stumble back, RICKY keeps wrapping the tape around.

JOANNE: Ricky, stop it!

KELISHA: Dad please, you're hurting him!

JOANNE: Let go of him now!

The men fall to the ground and RICKY traps RICHARD.

RICKY: Have you just come back to rip everyone away from me again?

JOANNE: Kelisha go outside!

KELISHA: Just make him stop!

RICKY: All right then. All right then, Richard. Poor Little Richard, gentle soul.

RICKY really shakes RICHARD, almost strangling him.

The day of Kelisha's first birthday. Can you remember that ey? I come back early from London to surprise my daughter. Seventy-two hours without sleep, working in the studio non-stop for me and you. Miranda nowhere to be seen. And I find you. In my bed. Not a stitch on. Chopping up white powder on a photo of Mum. That same stupid gormless look you've got on your face now. Big cow eyes looking up at me. With Kelisha asleep five foot away.

JOANNE: Come on, Kel, let's go through.

JOANNE tries to pull KELISHA but she won't budge.

RICKY: And you ran away Richard. You ran past me and down the stairs, out the front door and out of our life. And now you waltz back into it and you can't even remember any of it!

Laughter from the other room.

Cos there were plenty of times. Miranda said you both even tried to arrange an abortion before she had... *She* told me. When you'd gone. I made her. I *punched* her. I punched her in the face and she told me and I threw her out the house and told her never –

RICKY's back suddenly goes and he collapses on top of RICHARD. RICKY groans.

JOANNE: What are you doing to each other!?

RICKY: Aaargh!

JOANNE: You're gonna kill him!

RICKY: Me back. It's gone.

JOANNE: Stay still, Richard.

JOANNE helps to lift RICHARD. RICHARD slowly wriggles free. KELISHA tries to get past them. RICKY instantly grabs KELISHA's leg.

RICKY: No! Where you going!?

JOANNE: Ricky!

RICKY: Kelisha! Stay with me! Help me!

KELISHA uses all her strength to pull her leg away from his grip.

KELISHA: FUCK OFF!

KELISHA storms out through the back door.

Long pause.

JOANNE: Well done, Ricky. I think you handled that brilliantly.

JOANNE stands up, letting go of RICKY, who slumps and squirms in agony.

RICKY: I think I've done something.

JOANNE: Yeah I think you have.

RICKY: Is that it now, is it? I'm a monster to you now am I?

JOANNE: It's not me you should be worryin about.

RICKY: Get after her will ya!

JOANNE: Why?

RICKY: We don't know where she's gone! Anything could happen!

JOANNE: Oh and she's safer in here is she?

Beat.

RICKY: Maybe she was telling you to fuck off an' all.

Beat.

JOANNE: What's goin on in that head of yours, Ricky? You're just so full of... It's beyond bitter. It's *poison.*

Beat.

After everything I've been through with... You'd rather lie through your teeth all this time than confide in me.

Beat.

Why can't you *talk* to me?

JOANNE sees she's not going to get an answer and goes to leave.

RICKY: Will you take me home?

Beat.

JOANNE: I'm gonna go down there. I'm gonna talk to some people who'll have a laugh with me, get me a drink, have a dance and a sing, say well done for tryna make something of myself while I'm just about young enough. People who'll tell me the *truth.*

RICKY: Oh you'd know all about that, wouldn't you?

Beat.

JOANNE: That's it, Ricky. You just lie there and stew in your own juice.

JOANNE grabs her drink and exits to the cellar. The sound of cheering from below as 'Down Down' by Status Quo kicks in.

RICKY is on his knees. RICHARD is slumped against a cupboard. They can't look at each other. Both dead still.

The music lifts into...

SCENE SEVEN

Saturday (four hours later). 3 am. Grass verge opposite JOANNE's house.

It is raining hard. KELISHA enters, hammered. She is soaked through. She has a can of Stella. She dials on her mobile.

RICHARD enters. He is extremely cautious, following KELISHA but making sure he's not seen.

KELISHA: (*On the phone.*) Hello Joanne. It's me, Little Miss... FREAK! You horrible slaggy...scally... It's Kelisha by the way. I'm so sorry to disturb ya, I know you're all busy at the party together...but I'm just lettin you know...I'm goin. I'm getting me stuff and I'm goin. And so can you tell me dad... sorry DADZ...tell me DADZZZ...

She laughs.

You can tell them too.

Beat.

And you can tell them I've just been with the oompa loompa lad. He saw me leaving and came after me to see I was all right. More than any of you lot did.

Beat.

And d'ya know what I did? I got in his shitty suped up car and he drove me to the beach, and we had a bottle of voddie, and I had sex with him.

Beat.

I'm goin now, and I'm gonna set fire to the house and I hope I never see any of you lying horrible...EVER again.

Beat.

But I gave Richard me key so come and let me in. Now. Okay? Okay bye now. Tarra.

RICHARD has been approaching slowly. He touches KELISHA's shoulder. She screams in shock and drops the phone. RICHARD freezes.

RICHARD: Kelisha, it's me! It's Richard!

KELISHA stands.

KELISHA: What ya doing?

RICHARD: Nothing, I've…nothing! Are you okay? You're soaked.

KELISHA: Where's me keys? Where are they?

RICHARD: I –

KELISHA: Give me them. Where's the other two, are you all watching me ey?

RICHARD: No! I'm on my own.

Beat.

Ricky's gone to hospital.

Beat.

Joanne stayed at the party.

Beat.

You're all wet.

He strokes her hair.

Beat.

You need to get –

KELISHA: Good party wasn't it?

RICHARD: Um. Yeah it was –

KELISHA: They loved you didn't they?

RICHARD: Where've you been?

KELISHA: With some lads. Loads of them. And now I'm locked out. Drenched. Bladdered. On me own.

Beat.

Not much of a dad are ya?

RICHARD takes off his jacket and tries to put it on KELISHA's shoulder. She flings it off.

There's nothing *wrong* with your memory –

RICHARD: There is!

KELISHA: All this time you've been pretending to be my friend, you *knew* –

RICHARD: No!

KELISHA: You knew and there's nothing wrong with you at all –

RICHARD: I can't tell you anything Kelisha! I can't even *think* straight. What do you think it's like for me? I feel like I don't know who I am!

KELISHA: Well what about me! I'm just a complete and utter mistake who shouldn't have been born!

Beat.

I wanna go and find her.

RICHARD: Who?

KELISHA: *Her.*

RICHARD: Miranda?

KELISHA: 'Miranda.'

RICHARD: I don't know wher –

KELISHA: LIAR!

RICHARD: What do you want her for?

KELISHA: She's my mum, isn't she!? I've met you now, so I may as well meet her and let her laugh at me. And when she does *I'll* punch her face in too, she deserved it, she still does! So do you!

She starts hitting RICHARD's chest.

Why's it taken you seventeen years and a bang on the head to come and see your own daughter?

She starts smacking his head.

Why!?

RICHARD: No, stop it!

KELISHA: Well you're here now, so come on. What ya gonna do about it? We can't stay here. Where you gonna take me?

RICHARD: I can't –

KELISHA: You've got to! Have you got money?

RICHARD: No –

KELISHA: Can you get some?

She picks up his coat and digs into his pockets.

What's all this then?

RICHARD: It's my passport and –

KELISHA: You can get someone to fly us over there.

She rummages through the coat again.

Where's me key? Gimme it.

RICHARD gets it from his trousers pocket.

RICHARD: It's here. You'd need a passport too though and –

KELISHA: I've got one. And a rucksack. I've got a travel plug too.
We'll take the sleeping bag. I can stay with your people in
Amsterdam. You can sort me a job in one of your cafés, I've
got experience. Come on! I can do what the HELL I want
now! There's nothing stopping me!

JOANNE enters. She is wearing a Viking hat.

JOANNE: What's going on?

Beat.

Are you okay Kel?

Beat.

RICHARD: She's fine.

JOANNE: What are you doing here Richard?

RICHARD: I'm making sure Kelisha's all right.

JOANNE: I thought you were going the hospital?

RICHARD: He went mad in the taxi. I got out.

Beat.

JOANNE: Kelisha, look at you. What are you leaving me messages
like that for? Where've you been?

JOANNE goes to touch her.

Kelish –

KELISHA: Don't touch me! Don't ever touch me again!

KELISHA exits to the house.

JOANNE: Kelisha!

Pause.

What have you said to her?

Pause.

You're gonna have to go now, Richard.

RICHARD: I'm waiting for Kelisha.

Beat.

JOANNE: That your coat?

JOANNE picks up RICHARD's coat. She holds it to him. He stands still.

Put it on.

He doesn't move. She lets it drop to the floor. She gets some cash from her coat pocket.

RICHARD: She wants to come with me.

JOANNE: Put it on.

RICHARD holds her stare. JOANNE takes his hand and puts the cash in.

Beat.

RICHARD: How much is that?

JOANNE: Enough. You're going *now* though.

RICHARD picks up his coat, puts it on.

Buses start in two hours. Go the airport.

JOANNE does one of his buttons, checks his woolly hat, pats one of his pockets.

RICHARD: My bag –

JOANNE: No. I'll sling it. Go now.

RICHARD zips up his coat, waits, walks away.

Richard.

RICHARD stops.

Don't come back.

Beat.

RICHARD: Tell Ricky…

Beat.

Tell Kelisha –

JOANNE: Bye Richard.

RICHARD exits.

Pause.

JOANNE picks up the can of lager and enters the house. KELISHA is wearing a coat and carrying a cartoonish kids day sack.

Kelisha. Come and –

KELISHA: Where is he?

JOANNE: He's gone.

KELISHA: I'm going with him! Richard!

JOANNE: You're not going anywhere Kel –

KELISHA: Don't tell *me*! Which way did he…

KELISHA goes to leave. JOANNE tackles her. KELISHA screams and breaks down.

No!

JOANNE: Kel!

KELISHA: Get off!

JOANNE: Oi!

KELISHA: You're not my –

JOANNE: Stop it!

KELISHA: No!

JOANNE: Kelisha!

KELISHA: LEAVE ME ALONE!

She slumps onto the floor.

JOANNE: Kelisha.

Beat.

KELISHA: I've got no one!

Beat.

JOANNE: Kel. Here. Look at me.

KELISHA: No!

JOANNE: You're soaked, you'll catch ya death.

KELISHA: I feel sick.

JOANNE: Well get it up then. Don't hold it in. Come on.

KELISHA: No! I'm not moving anywhere, not yet!

JOANNE: Okay, okay.

KELISHA vomits.

KELISHA: Ugh! No!

JOANNE: It's okay, it's okay Kel! You can…just, let it… We'll clean it up.

JOANNE stands, helpless.

Of course you haven't got no one. I'm here now aren't I?

Beat.

And you've got your dad.

Beat.

Ricky's your dad.

Beat.

Who's the man who's cleaned up after ya all these years, even before I knew ya?

Beat.

He'd do it now.

Beat.

If he was here.

KELISHA can't relax. She is breathing heavily, almost using her voice to breathe.

SCENE EIGHT

Saturday (three hours later) 6 am. Living Room.

A body is slumped on the sofa, completely covered by a sleeping bag.

RICKY enters with a metal walking stick. He is wearing a back support which is just about visible under his shirt from the party. He is in extreme pain and walks very, very slowly. He calls upstairs.

RICKY: Hello?

Beat.

Joanne? Can you come down? I need…money! For the taxi!

Pause.

He's outside! He's waiting!

RICKY turns round, peers outside, slight wave.

Beat.

I need to pay him!

Beat.

There's money in me coat pocket, on the floor!

Beat.

Hello? Can you bring –

KELISHA bursts in quickly wearing pyjamas. She carries a money box which jingles full of coins.

Kel. Hi love. Here d'ya want me to…

KELISHA is past him, heading outside.

Wait, what are ya…I'll go…don't give him a tip!

He notices the sleeping bag. He goes to it and stands over it.

Pause.

Richard.

Pause.

He touches the bag with his stick. The bag is soft. He scoops back one end and sees nobody is underneath. RICKY thinks, then chucks his stick on the floor.

KELISHA re-enters. RICKY hears her behind him, arches his neck to see her.

Kelisha?

RICKY turns 180° to see her, painfully slowly.

Darlin.

Beat.

Where's Jo? She in bed?

Beat.

Where's…he's not here is he?

Pause.

I've escaped. The nurse went off to get someone and I made a run for it. Well, not a run exactly…

Fake laugh.

You sitting down?

Beat.

Think *I* will. Can you help me on here?

Beat. RICKY sees he isn't going to get any help, so he sets about trying to collapse himself onto the sofa. He can't hide his slowness, but he does everything in his power to not moan or show pain in his face, which only serves to make him look even more distressed.

He finally gets onto the couch. He is shaking. Vulnerable. Eyes trying to see what KELISHA is doing. He grabs the sleeping bag. He is lying on his back.

Nippy innit? You want some of this? Come on it's cold, get under here Kel.

Beat.

I mean, that's if…if you want to, like.

Beat. RICKY covers his lower half with the sleeping bag.

Kelisha. Will you…at least sit close to me.

Beat.

KELISHA sits cross-legged where she is, in the middle of the floor.

I can't see you.

KELISHA empties her money box and starts counting out her coins.

You been asleep?

KELISHA pauses, looks at him, 'what do you think?', continues counting.

Pause.

Cabbie didn't help me once. Just stared at me in his mirror. Chewin. I was tryna open the door and –

KELISHA: My whole life I thought she'd abandoned me. You don't know how horrible that is. Hardly any of the kids in my class had a mum *and* a dad, but at least they had a *mum*. What kind of kid doesn't live with their mum! And not even a dead mum so people'd feel sorry for me. Like *you* had.

Beat.

When Jo used to pick me up from school, all the other kids'd think she was me sister, and they'd say, 'Why's she a different colour, does your mum put it about?' But they were right, weren't they? She did put it about didn't she?

Beat.

That sofa you're lying on. That he's been sleepin on. I made us bring that here when we moved in with Jo, cos you said that was what me mum left me on. With a note pinned to me like I was a parcel, you said. So I wanted to keep the sofa. And you let me. How could you let me believe that?

RICKY: When was the right time Kelisha? You were just a baby, then suddenly you're four, then five, then six, then ten, then a teenager. How do I break something like that? Where do you go to learn that, to do the right thing?

KELISHA: Well you don't just keep running away. Look at you. You've even just ran away from the hospital. You need help. The longer you leave something the worse it's gonna get.

Beat.

Have you always been…like *this?*

Beat.

RICKY: I had my head in the clouds for *years.* All I wanted was to be the big cheese. And be a million miles from here. Never doubted it. Was gonna happen. It *was* happening. Never gave a second thought to all the people around me.

Beat.

And look what really happens.

Beat.

She was twenty-one last time I saw her. Your mum.

Beat.

Looked just like you.

Beat.

But she was nothing *like* you. That's why you're so… I can't explain… She just… She was a *taker.* Didn't care about us. Just came along for the ride.

Beat.

And then I was on me own.

KELISHA: Well maybe you could have *made* it on your own.

RICKY: Well maybe I wasn't good enough!

KELISHA: How do you know!? You've never *tried!*

Beat.

RICKY: All I care about now…is not letting anything happen to you that could hurt ya –

KELISHA: Like what!? Let *what* happen to me!? You don't ever *let* anything happen to me! Because I can't go anywhere! What do I do then, stay under this roof for the next fifty years, sit on that couch, watch that telly, just me and you, block the world out! I need to live, I need to have a life! I *want* to.

Beat.

And so should you Dad.

Beat.

Look at you.

Beat.

RICKY: Who's to say I haven't made something of my life. What more could I want than sharing a home with you?

Beat.

KELISHA: And Joanne?

Pause.

You think that's still gonna happen?

RICKY: Why wouldn't it?

Beat.

KELISHA: I just wanna go as well. I'll probably hate uni but so what. No one'll know who I am there. I can just lie. I can just do what you've all done. Make them think I'm normal.

The synth from 'This is the Day' by The The fades up. The song kicks in and plays into…

SCENE NINE

Thursday (five days later). 10 am. Living room.

The PA system is in the room. RICKY is sitting on the sofa.

KELISHA enters and sits on the arm. She is wearing a DIY-4-U t-shirt. They are watching the TV, which is on mute. They don't look at each other. RICKY has his microphone.

RICKY: (*Over the mic.*) Hello, hello, hello.

Pause.

KELISHA: This the right channel?

RICKY: Yeah. D'ya want the sound on?

KELISHA: Nah. Nothing on.

Beat.

Think I'll have a cuppa.

RICKY: I'll do this one.

KELISHA: You don't have to, Dad.

RICKY: I *wannoo.*

RICKY stands slowly. KELISHA helps him. He walks off to the kitchen.

RICKY exits.

Pause.

KELISHA: Dad! Here it is again!

RICKY: (*Off.*) What?

KELISHA: The advert! Joanne's on the telly!

KELISHA jumps up to get the remote control.

RICKY: (*Off.*) Oh I'll…I'll see it next time.

Beat.

KELISHA is standing next to the phone. She presses play on the answer phone. The test message from Scene Four plays. 'Message One: One-two. Hello. It's Richard. Little Richard. Not sure what I should say. I'm on my own. Everyone else is…somewhere else. I think everything is looking okay. I hope so anyway. It will be as long as you're listening to this. Peace and love. Bye.'

KELISHA thinks, then presses delete.

JOANNE enters from the front door. She is dressed in her new flight attendant uniform and wiping her hands on an oily rag.

JOANNE: Stupid ald banger.

KELISHA: Jo! You just missed it again!

JOANNE: Ah. Never mind.

Beat.

KELISHA: Is it all right?

JOANNE: Yeah, just stinks.

KELISHA: Reckon it'll get you down and back?

JOANNE: Long as it gets me down.

Beat.

Y'okay?

KELISHA: Just worried they'll put me on the till.

JOANNE: They won't, I've told them. You're just an extra pair of eyes to cover me while I've got me training, don't worry. My t-shirt fit you all right?

KELISHA: Yeah. Can't get this stain out though.

JOANNE: Oh yeah, sorry. Think it's kebab sauce. I just hide it with me fob.

Beat.

Reckon I'll buy a new car. Soon as I get my first wages. Won't hardly need it when I'm away though.

Beat.

Get you on it.

KELISHA: Me?

JOANNE: Get you some lessons. I couldn't wait when I was your age.

KELISHA: I've never thought about it.

JOANNE: We'll *do* it. I'll take you out, get you started. Down the dock road. In the evenings when I'm home. Still be light. Nice and quiet. Have you driving by the end of the summer.

Beat.

Then you'll be gone.

Beat.

Won't ya?

RICKY re-enters.

Won't she?

RICKY: Won't she what?

JOANNE: Be living away by the end of the summer?

RICKY: That's not my decision.

JOANNE: What would be your decision?

Beat.

RICKY: My decision is…that it's not my decision.

JOANNE: Really?

RICKY: It's been decided.

JOANNE: Kel?

KELISHA: Look, I haven't made me mind up yet, okay? I've still gotta do me exams. And then…I'll do what *I* wanna do. There's a whole summer to come. Can't we have that first?

Beat.

Just…please. Leave it alone till then.

KELISHA puts on her headphones.

Pause.

RICKY: What do you want me to say Joanne?

Beat.

I'm scared. I'm scared of you leaving and never coming back. Same with her.

JOANNE: It's a job, that's all. A good one. A better one. Better for me.

RICKY: I know.

JOANNE: Well then. Instead of animosity and jealousy, after all that's happened, I wouldn't mind a pat on the back.

Beat.

RICKY: What, from here? Who d'ya think I am, Mr Tickle?

KELISHA: HEY DAD! CAN YOU HEAR ME? GUESS WHAT SONG I'VE GOT ON THIS? YOUR ONE! DO YOU WANNA LISTEN?

RICKY shakes his head.

JO?

JOANNE shakes her head.

Pause.

JOANNE: I haven't done anything wrong here. I'm the one who should be scared. You've gotta prove to me you think we've got something worth saving.

RICKY picks up the gong and stares at it.

RICKY: D'ya wanna practise your interview?

Beat.

JOANNE: Yeah, I would. That'd be great.

RICKY: But I've got the gong, so you can't say yes or no.

Pause.

What's your name?

Beat.

JOANNE: Joanne.

RICKY: Joanne what?

JOANNE: Joanne Jenkins.

RICKY: Where you from?

JOANNE: Liverpool.

RICKY: Liverpool?

JOANNE: That's right.

RICKY: What's your current annual income?

JOANNE: Not enough.

RICKY: Have you flown many times?

JOANNE: Not for years.

RICKY: Did you like being on a plane?

JOANNE: I tend to fall asleep.

RICKY: Are you married?

JOANNE: I have a partner.

RICKY: Is he…a good lover?

JOANNE: I tend to fall asleep.

RICKY: What's his name?

JOANNE: Ricky.

RICKY: Ricky who?

JOANNE: Ricky Hill.

RICKY: Ricky Hill?

JOANNE: Ricky Hill.

Beat.

RICKY: What does he do?

Beat.

JOANNE: He used to do a lot of things.

JOANNE is blowing her nails dry across her mouth.

RICKY: Do you know you've dropped your harmonica?

Beat.

Did you just nod your head?

JOANNE: Nnnn…not at all.

RICKY: You sure?

JOANNE: Positive.

Beat.

RICKY: Would you marry him?

JOANNE: Good one.

RICKY: Would you though?

JOANNE: He's never asked me.

RICKY: Would you marry him?

Beat.

JOANNE: Yes.

RICKY bangs the gong. He exits upstairs.

Pause.

JOANNE starts applying make-up.

Beat.

Kelisha. Kel.

JOANNE puts down her make-up.

Come on Kel…

Beat.

I'm gonna make a move now, Kel.

Beat.

Kelisha.

Beat.

Can you hear me?

JOANNE goes over to KELISHA and puts an arm on her shoulder.

KELISHA: God Jo! You scared the wotsits outta me!

Beat.

You look nice.

KELISHA looks up at JOANNE, smiling.

Gotta put loadsa slap on, ey?

Beat.

No – you look great.

Beat.

Reckon I could have some?

JOANNE: You?

KELISHA: Why not?

JOANNE: Since when have you worn make-up?

KELISHA: Since now. Just a little bit.

Beat.

JOANNE: All right then. Sit up straight.

KELISHA sits facing JOANNE. KELISHA's top has JOANNE 4 U on the back in football name and numbering style.

If you're thinking of copping off with Sid, he's married.

KELISHA: Shurrup.

Beat.

What do I do?

Beat.

JOANNE: Close your eyes.

JOANNE starts applying make up to KELISHA.

I'll drop you off if you want.

KELISHA: It's okay. I can walk.

Beat.

I've got spots. All this stress lately.

JOANNE: You have not. Wish I had your skin.

The sound of RICKY peeing in the bathroom is heard through the speakers.

RICKY: (*Off, over the mic.*) Ol' man river, that ol' man river. He must know something, but don't say nothing.

KELISHA: How many times is he going to do that and think it's funny?

Pause.

Don't go, Jo.

JOANNE stops doing the make-up. KELISHA opens her eyes.

Don't leave us.

Beat.

JOANNE finishes with the make-up.

JOANNE: All done.

JOANNE stands.

KELISHA: Where you going?

Beat.

JOANNE: Just gonna say tarra to ya dad.

JOANNE walks away.

KELISHA: Just…tarra? Or *goodbye*?

JOANNE stops.

JOANNE: Just tarra.

JOANNE exits.

KELISHA sits.

End.

www.ingramcontent.com/pod-product-compliance
Ingram Content Group UK Ltd.
Pitfield, Milton Keynes, MK11 3LW, UK
UKHW020724280225
455688UK00012B/498